THE BEDFORD SERIES IN HISTORY AND CULTURE

The Secret

by Francesco Petrarch

WITH RELATED DOCUMENTS

Related Titles in
THE BEDFORD SERIES IN HISTORY AND CULTURE
Advisory Editors: Natalie Zemon Davis, Princeton University
Ernest R. May, Harvard University
Lynn Hunt, University of California, Los Angeles
David W. Blight, Yale University

THE BEDFORD SERIES IN HISTORY AND CULTURE

The Secret

by Francesco Petrarch

WITH RELATED DOCUMENTS

Edited with an Introduction by

Carol E. Quillen

Rice University

BEDFORD/ST. MARTIN'S   Boston ◆ New York

For Bedford/St. Martin's

Publisher for History: Patricia A. Rossi
Director of Development for History: Jane Knetzger
Developmental Editor: Rachel L. Safer
Associate Editor, Publishing Services: Maria Teresa Burwell
Production Supervisor: Jennifer Wetzel
Marketing Manager: Jenna Bookin Barry
Project Management: Books By Design, Inc.
Text Design: Claire Seng-Niemoeller
Indexer: Books By Design, Inc.
Cover Design: Billy Boardman
Cover Art: Portrait of Petrarch (Manuscript Detail). From the Collection of Laurenziana
    Medicea Library, Florence. Courtesy of the Ministry of Cultural Assets.
Composition: Stratford Publishing Services, Inc.
Printing and Binding: Haddon Craftsmen, an RR Donnelley & Sons Company

President: Joan E. Feinberg
Editorial Director: Denise B. Wydra
Director of Marketing: Karen R. Melton
Director of Editing, Design, and Production: Marcia Cohen
Manager, Publishing Services: Emily Berleth

Library of Congress Control Number: 2002111604

Manufactured in the United States of America.

8   7   6
f   e   d   c   b

For information, write: Bedford / St. Martin's, 75 Arlington Street, Boston, MA 02116
(617-399-4000)

ISBN: 0-312-15438-0

Acknowledgments

From *Aeneid* by Virgil, translated by Robert Fitzgerald, copyright © 1980, 1982, 1983 by
Robert Fitzgerald. Used by permission of Random House, Inc.

Map 1 from *The Making of the West: Peoples and Cultures* by Lynn Hunt, Thomas R.
Martin, Barbara H. Rosenwein, R. Po-chia Hsia, and Bonnie G. Smith. Copyright © 2001
by Bedford / St. Martin's.

Map 3 adapted from *The Making of the West: Peoples and Cultures* by Lynn Hunt,
Thomas R. Martin, Barbara H. Rosenwein, R. Po-chia Hsia, and Bonnie G. Smith.
Copyright © 2001 by Bedford / St. Martin's.

Foreword

The Bedford Series in History and Culture is designed so that readers can study the past as historians do.

The historian's first task is finding the evidence. Documents, letters, memoirs, interviews, pictures, movies, novels, or poems can provide facts and clues. Then the historian questions and compares the sources. There is more to do than in a courtroom, for hearsay evidence is welcome, and the historian is usually looking for answers beyond act and motive. Different views of an event may be as important as a single verdict. How a story is told may yield as much information as what it says.

Along the way the historian seeks help from other historians and perhaps from specialists in other disciplines. Finally, it is time to write, to decide on an interpretation and how to arrange the evidence for readers.

Each book in this series contains an important historical document or group of documents, each document a witness from the past and open to interpretation in different ways. The documents are combined with some element of historical narrative—an introduction or a biographical essay, for example—that provides students with an analysis of the primary source material and important background information about the world in which it was produced.

Each book in the series focuses on a specific topic within a specific historical period. Each provides a basis for lively thought and discussion about several aspects of the topic and the historian's role. Each is short enough (and inexpensive enough) to be a reasonable one-week assignment in a college course. Whether as classroom or personal reading, each book in the series provides firsthand experience of the challenge—and fun—of discovering, recreating, and interpreting the past.

Natalie Zemon Davis
Ernest R. May
Lynn Hunt
David W. Blight

Preface

Important books can have unpredictable histories. In the prologue to *The Secret,* Francesco Petrarch sets this dialogue apart from his other works, stating that although he seeks public acclaim for most of his writings, *The Secret* has no intended audience; it is to remain a private source of memories and pleasure for its author alone. Yet this ostensibly private work has attracted more readers and received far more scholarly attention than most of Petrarch's Latin writings. Such fame, though perhaps unsought, is surely warranted. More than any other text, and in spite of its resonances with medieval literary traditions, this "secret" account of one man's inner struggles reveals the aspirations and methods of the broad and profoundly influential humanist movement.

Although critics and historians agree on *The Secret*'s importance, they have fiercely debated its precise meaning and significance for centuries. Petrarch's text indisputably records an imagined conversation between two interlocutors named Franciscus, modeled on Petrarch, and Augustinus, modeled on the Latin church father Augustine (354–430). Beyond this, readers agree on little. Whereas some readers understand *The Secret* as indicative of the perennial conflict that humanists felt between their love for pagan literature and their Christian obligations, others see it as one individual's response to a specific moral crisis. Some find recounted in *The Secret* both a kind of autobiographical conversion and a plan for a more religious future, whereas others view it as a work of pure fiction. To some, *The Secret* clearly reveals the fears and preoccupations of a late medieval man; to others, it triumphantly heralds the birth of a new kind of self and a more secular age. This book that was aimed at no audience (some readers wonder whether Petrarch meant what he said) has in fact garnered a large and contentious one. As a result, *The Secret* has become central within many areas of inquiry: the history of reading, the emergence of the intellectual as a social type, the relationship in the West between

Greco-Roman cultures and Judeo-Christian traditions, and the rise of individualism.

Most significantly, Petrarch's dialogue is central, indeed indispensable, to any understanding of the humanist movement and the revival of antiquity that so shaped many facets of early modern European culture. *The Secret* of course attests to Petrarch's passion for classical Greece and Rome. Even more than this, it demonstrates how he thought writings from the distant past could serve the needs of his very different culture. Indeed, *The Secret* offers one of the strongest justifications for humanism that Petrarch, that movement's canonical father, ever wrote.

This volume aims to make *The Secret* accessible to students in a way that allows them to grapple with its historical significance. To this end, the first part of the introduction outlines the milieu in which Renaissance humanism emerged and flourished, situating the desire to revive antiquity within the context of Italian city-states during the thirteenth and fourteenth centuries. The introduction then describes the specific activities through which Petrarch and his followers recovered the past, thereby defining humanism as a set of practices as well as a cultural ideal. Finally, because the term *humanism* came to mean much more than the revival of antiquity, this section suggests some possible connections between Petrarch's ideals and activities and later intellectual movements.

The Secret is a complex and at times contradictory text, one that questions the value of the humanist project even as it authorizes it. The second part of the introduction describes some of these complexities, focusing particularly on the discrepancy between the Augustinus of *The Secret* and the historical Augustine and on the irresolute ending of the dialogue. Although the introduction takes an interpretive stand, it does not attempt to resolve contradictions or to simplify complexities that are inherent in this text. Rather, it aims to invite readers to engage this rewarding text for themselves.

In addition to *The Secret,* this volume includes excerpts from four related texts: Petrarch's first letter to Cicero, from his *Familiar Letters;* the conversion scene from Augustine's *Confessions;* a passage from Virgil's *Aeneid;* and a passage from Augustine's *City of God.* The first selection concisely illustrates the intimate tone that Petrarch used with ancient writers. The remaining three excerpts allow students to compare ancient texts with Petrarch's use of them in *The Secret* and thus to gain insight into the complex structure of this dialogue. Finally, this book includes a glossary of names contained in the dialogue as well as in the introduction and notes, a brief chronology of key events in Petrarch's life, suggested questions for discussion, and an annotated bibliography to help students think critically about Francesco Petrarch, *The Secret,* and humanism.

ACKNOWLEDGMENTS

I am grateful to Natalie Zemon Davis, who initially encouraged this project, and to Lynn Hunt, advisory editor for the Bedford Series in History and Culture. Without the help and patience of the fine editors at Bedford/St. Martin's, I would not have finished this volume. I am especially grateful to Patricia A. Rossi, publisher for history, and Rachel L. Safer, my developmental editor. I thank the superb scholars who generously read part or all of the manuscript: Joseph Byrne, Belmont University; Joan Coffey, Sam Houston State University; Arthur Field, University of Indiana; Anthony Grafton, Princeton University; Donald Kelley, Rutgers University; Michael Maas, Rice University; John Najemy, Cornell University; Duane Osheim, University of Virginia; Paula Sanders, Rice University; and others who read the manuscript at and for the press. Catherine Howard produced an initial draft of the glossary and provided important editorial help. Ruth Anne Johnson reviewed the entire translation, saving me from many errors and vastly improving the quality and accuracy of this text. She has my warmest thanks.

The comments, corrections, and suggestions of these generous scholars have immeasurably improved this book. Any errors that remain are entirely my own.

Carol E. Quillen

Contents

Maps and Illustrations

PART ONE

Introduction: Petrarch's *Secret* and Renaissance Humanism

Francesco Petrarch (1304–1374) was the most famous writer of his time. A gifted Italian poet, he also took the lead among his contemporaries in inaugurating the "revival of antiquity," or what historians now call the humanist movement. Humanists were writers and scholars in the fourteenth, fifteenth, and sixteenth centuries who sought to recover and emulate the literature of ancient Rome and later of ancient Greece. Their enthusiasm for classical and early Christian culture shaped literary and artistic production in Europe for hundreds of years.

The Secret (also called *The Secret Conflict of My Cares*), written in Latin in the mid-fourteenth century, attests to and explains Petrarch's passion for antiquity and illustrates his formative influence on the humanist movement. Indeed, this work shows how literature both from very distant ages (from the first century B.C.E. through the fourth century C.E.) and from different cultures (republican, imperial, and early Christian Rome) that was written in the difficult, alien language of classical Latin, could serve the needs of Petrarch's own day. In other words, *The Secret* offers one of the clearest justifications for the revival of antiquity that Petrarch, the father of that revival, ever wrote. As such, it is a central text for understanding European culture in the

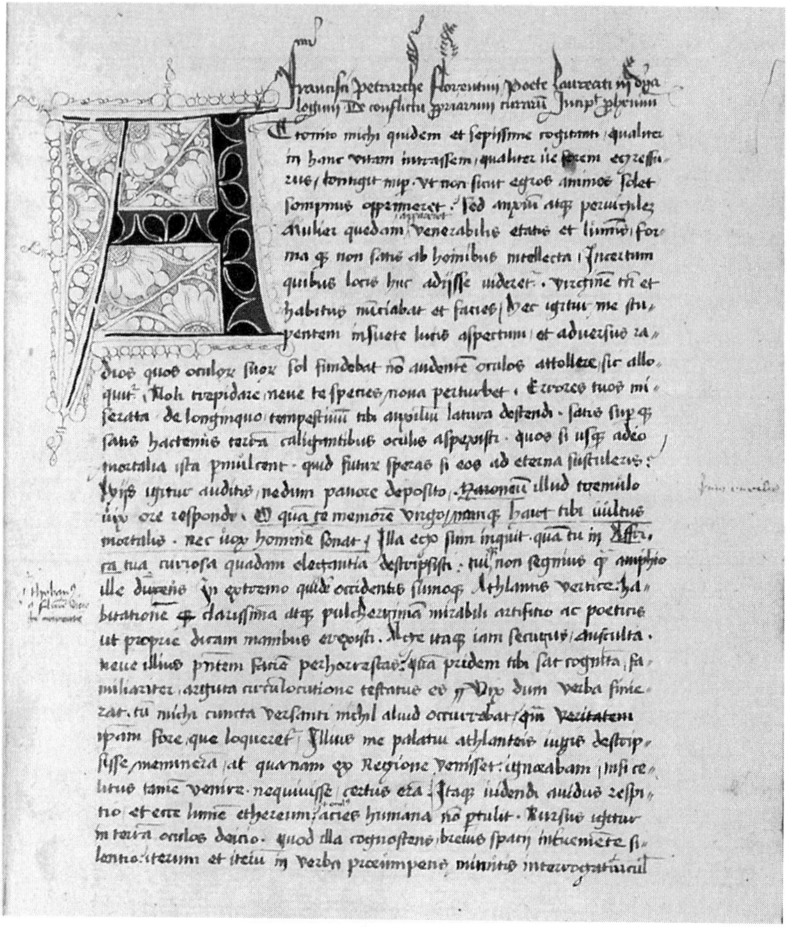

Figure 1.   Opening of *The Secret*.

This folio, written in the Netherlands in the fifteenth century, comes from the only Latin manuscript of *The Secret* that is now housed in the United States.

Petrarca, *Secretum* #4648, Bd Ms 31+. Northern France ca. 1450, Division of Rare and Manuscript Collections, Cornell University Library. Paper.

early modern period (roughly 1350–1600), the era called (somewhat controversially) the Renaissance. Furthermore, because the Renaissance represents, as nineteenth-century historian Jacob Burckhardt famously wrote, a culture that in some ways gave rise to our own, *The Secret* also helps us to understand the emergence of "modernity" and its still powerful legacies.

The primary aim of this introduction is to provide the background necessary to allow for an informed, rewarding reading of *The Secret*. Toward this end, the following pages discuss the context in which humanist practices emerged in thirteenth- and fourteenth-century Italy, Petrarch's role in the dissemination of humanist ideas and practices, the enduring historical significance of the Renaissance humanist movement, and the importance of *The Secret* as a humanist text.

PETRARCH AND THE HUMANIST MOVEMENT

A Crown for a Poet

On April 8, 1341, Francesco Petrarca (in English, Petrarch) was proclaimed poet laureate by the senate and people of Rome. The ceremony took place on the Capitoline Hill, an ancient center of Roman civic life, amid ruins that dated back to the city's founding in the eighth century B.C.E. As he stood in this historic place, Petrarch imagined that his coronation echoed a ritual from the heyday of the Roman Empire, when (or so he thought) every five years contests were held to acknowledge authors of extraordinary talent. By pursuing such an honor for himself more than a thousand years later, Petrarch, a poet and scholar, sought a kind of recognition that crossed the centuries to connect him and his activities as a writer to writers from antiquity.

To judge by his reputation both in the fourteenth century and now, Petrarch deserved the laurel crown he received on that day. During his lifetime, he was arguably the most famous writer in Europe, and today, more than six hundred years later, we still recognize him as an exceptional scholar and poet. Of his voluminous works — some written in Latin, some in Italian — his Italian lyric poetry has best retained its popularity. Indeed, his *Rime sparse* (also called the *Canzoniere;* in English, *Scattered Verse*), a collection of love poems in Italian inspired by a mysterious woman named Laura, remains beloved. The themes of these poems — sublimated desire, the relationship between writing and feeling, the costs of authorship, the struggle for self-discovery — appeal to modern readers with startling immediacy. To the extent that he has achieved lasting glory, Petrarch owes his success to these vernacular writings.

Today many celebrate Petrarch for his Italian lyric poems. Yet at the time of his coronation, Petrarch assumed that his fame would ultimately depend on his Latin, not his Italian, works. He specifically sought out a ceremony that acknowledged his connection to ancient Roman authors who wrote in Latin. Among his own writings, he had especially high hopes for two unfinished works: his great work of historical biography, *De viris illustribus* (in English, *On Famous Men*); and his Latin epic poem *Africa,* about Scipio Africanus (ca. 236–183 B.C.E.), a hero of the Second Punic War (218–201 B.C.E.), during which Rome defeated Hannibal (ca. 247–181 B.C.E.) and the city of Carthage. Furthermore, Petrarch delivered his coronation speech in Latin. He took as his starting point lines from the *Eclogues* of the Roman poet Virgil (70–19 B.C.E.) and throughout relied heavily on classical references, allusions, and quotations. As a whole, then, Petrarch's coronation attests less to his talent as an Italian poet than to his humanism—that is, to his passion for the history, literature, and cultural standards of republican and imperial Rome.

Few now read either *On Famous Men* or *Africa,* yet we continue to acknowledge Petrarch's crucial historical significance as the father of the humanist movement—as the man who in the fourteenth century began the effort to recover the literary and cultural standards expressed in classical texts. Petrarch earned this reputation as the first humanist even though his interest in the ancient world was not unprecedented. Others before him had certainly turned to Roman antiquity for inspiration and literary models. In particular, earlier thirteenth- and fourteenth-century writers in Italy, most notably Lovato dei Lovati (1241–1309) and Albertino Mussato (1261–1329), had appreciated the ancients. They had read many different kinds of writers: major Latin poets such as Ovid (ca. 43 B.C.E.–17 C.E.), Horace (65–8 B.C.E.), and Virgil; playwrights, especially Seneca (ca. 4 B.C.E.–65 C.E.); and historians, especially Sallust (ca. 86–34 B.C.E.). They had recognized the distinctiveness of classical genres, styles, and vocabulary, and they had produced work in Latin that imitated these distinctive attributes. Petrarch, however, surpassed his predecessors both in the range of activities he pursued to recover the distant Roman past and in his commitment to persuading others to follow his lead. His love of antiquity, which for him included early Christian cultures, took many forms: He enthusiastically collected, read, and critically edited ancient texts; he revived classical genres, particularly the personal letter and the dialogue, in his own work; he wrote letters to his favorite ancient (and long-dead) classical authors; he used his correspondence and other writing to cultivate a community of men who shared his passion for antiquity; and he insisted on the ethical value of classical studies by arguing for a connection between "eloquence," which he took to mean clarity and persuasive force as exemplified by ancient authors, and "virtue," defined as the capacity to lead a good human life.

Petrarch's *Secret* attests to these quintessentially humanist activities. In particular, it shows how Petrarch placed his humanistic studies—the critical reading and emulation of classical literature—in the service of a quest for virtue and salvation. As such, *The Secret* is a kind of humanist manifesto in which Petrarch makes clear why the study of ancient literature was so central to his conception of the good human life.

This introduction uses the term *humanism* primarily to refer to the practices through which Petrarch and his successors linked the ancient to the early modern world and thus the present to the distant past. These practices included collecting different versions of ancient texts, comparing them, and using the comparisons to determine the best versions; translating texts from Latin and, by the end of the fourteenth century, Greek; annotating ancient texts to help modern readers understand them; developing materials to teach classical stylistic norms to students learning Latin; compiling dictionaries and other aids to readers; exposing forgeries; and imitating the genres, rhetorical styles, vocabulary, and figures of speech of classical texts. Humanism was, in other words, a way of making the past relevant in the present. As such, it survived its first manifestation as a revival of antiquity in early modern Europe and persists today, shaping our ideas not only about scholarship and teaching, but also about the importance of history and about the relationship of the past to the present.

The Lure of the Past

Before turning specifically to Petrarch's role in the emergence of humanism, we must first ask why, from the thirteenth century on, some Italian writers found the distant past so interesting, so worthy of recovery and emulation. Why this new enthusiasm for antiquity, and why in the north-central Italian peninsula? After all, many artifacts and texts from the ancient world had remained known continuously from the decline of the Roman Empire through the Middle Ages. The writers whom Petrarch most admired—Cicero (106–43 B.C.E.), Virgil,

Seneca, and Augustine (354–430 C.E.) — had never been lost to western Europe. Therefore, we need to explain why, at this historical moment and in this place, a significant number of educated persons viewed texts and artifacts from antiquity in a new way, why they simultaneously began to seek them out, to imitate them, and to critically investigate them.

Here it is important to recall how this region of Italy differed in the later Middle Ages from other parts of western Europe (see Map 1). In spite of invasions and the disintegration of the western Roman Empire in the sixth century, areas in this part of Italy that had been cities never completely lost their urban heritage. Some civic traditions and some sense of connection to the ancient Roman world survived. Furthermore, these cities retained a central role first as the seats of bishops (cathedral cities) and later as administrative units within the territory claimed by Otto I (Holy Roman emperor from 962 to 973 C.E.) and his successors.

These episcopal cities, controlled by bishops and nominally under the authority of a distant emperor, emerged side by side with other relationships of allegiance that developed in the centuries following Rome's collapse, such as those between large, rural landowners (the emperor, the Catholic Church, powerful aristocratic families) and their tenants and proprietors. Since the seventeenth century, scholars have referred to these complex social relationships as feudalism or the feudal system. In northern Italy, feudalism (and serfdom, the agricultural labor system that often accompanied it) was shorter-lived than in some other parts of Europe, but it existed, and feudal relationships overlapped with urban and ecclesiastical structures of authority: Bishops were sometimes also counts of the Holy Roman Empire; key officials in episcopal cities might also hold land in the countryside from a local monastery; the emperor might address the inhabitants of an episcopal city directly as his subjects, conferring privileges or enacting special laws, or he might work through the bishop, treating him as their protector and lord. In times of crisis, when external threats were grave and the emperor weak and distant, bishops often acted independently to defend their cities.

As populations grew and the economy recovered and developed in the eleventh century, bishops who had basically become autonomous feudal-ecclesiastical rulers vied for power with other segments of the growing urban population, such as local landlords, neighboring bishops and princes, merchants, and artisans. These local struggles for power gave rise to communes, a new form of political association that first

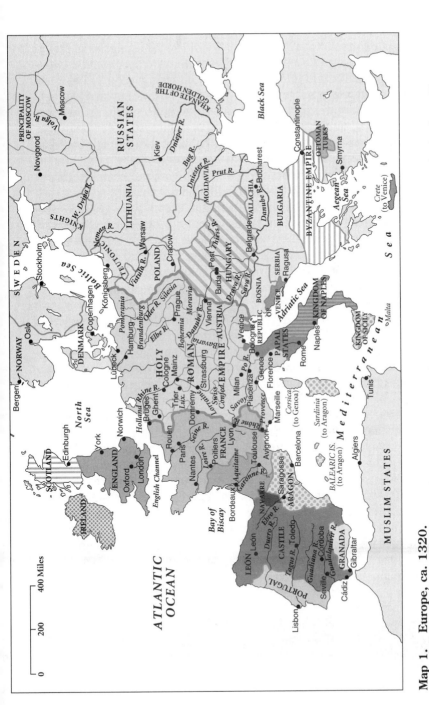

Map 1. Europe, ca. 1320.
In Italy north of Rome, city-states developed from earlier communes and fought to retain autonomy in the face of larger surrounding states.

emerged, sometimes with the support of the bishop, among prominent men living in diocesan towns in northern Italy. Communes were groups of men bound to each other by an oath of loyalty and by their common interest in peace and self-defense. Initially, they derived their authority from the separate prerogatives (to collect rent, enforce justice, defend territory) of their members, many of whom held land from the church or the emperor. Yet, between the eleventh and thirteenth centuries, these associations developed into a new form of political community, one that was different from the complex system of personal allegiances out of which it had emerged.

Broad comparisons of complex social phenomena always risk oversimplification. Nonetheless, it is important to recognize certain general differences between feudal and communal society. The communes that emerged in late medieval Italy encompassed feudal relations, but over time they produced a form of social organization that was different from a feudal system. Feudalism created a social order based on personal allegiance and reciprocal obligations between vassals and lords: Vassals promised to perform specified services for their lords, and in return lords granted to vassals tenure over income-producing land (fiefs). In such a system, allegiance is personal, and the obligations and power of individual vassals can vary widely. Communes, however, formed where men of high social standing could identify a common interest in the welfare of a particular city and its inhabitants. Over time, they came to foster a sense of the general, public good, and they created a space for shared decision making, where members could collectively deliberate on what was best for the community as a whole. This notion of "the public"—a space, an identity, and a good that differed from the space, identity, and good of any single person— encouraged the development of civic culture and civic pride. Furthermore, because in Italy the men who formed communes often held land in the countryside, the influence of these new associations extended beyond a city's walls. Indeed, the existence of communes contributed to the fragmentation of surrounding manorial estates, to the demise of serfdom, and to the rise of a wage labor system among peasants. Communes gradually assumed public authority and later legal jurisdiction in many urban areas in upper Italy. The civic and cultural institutions characteristic of early modern Italian city-states grew from these eleventh-century political communities.

Over the course of the twelfth and thirteenth centuries, Italian communal institutions grew more complex as each city incorporated more social groups and took on more public functions. However, political stability and autonomy remained fragile. Two dangers particularly threatened a city's independence: the intrusion of an external power, such as the pope, a territorial ruler, or a nearby city; and the rise to dominance within the city of a single family or faction. To ameliorate these threats, communes took two steps. First, they formed shifting alliances with other powers. Although these alliances initially pitted the pope and his allies (called the Guelf party) against the Holy Roman emperor and his allies (the Ghibelline party), over time the terms Guelf and Ghibelline lost their initial meanings and were used to describe many different alliances with many different agendas. By forging ties to other cities and rulers, communes strengthened their capacity to withstand threats from external powers. Second, to prevent a single family or faction from gaining too much influence, communes developed advisory councils representing different groups within the city, complicated selection processes for office-holders, and specific governmental positions that could be occupied only by outsiders. Although these strategies did not always work—single families or parties began to dominate many Italian communes as early as 1300—they did allow for the development of a new kind of civic life and culture.

The communes that flourished in Italy from the eleventh century on provided a context for the development of a complex, cosmopolitan milieu whose social and institutional needs differed from those of feudal lords or territorial princes. Communes needed procedures for collective decision making and rules for deciding who could participate. They needed courts to resolve conflicts among their members, legislative assemblies to make laws, some provision for collective defense, and a way to raise money to pay for these things. They needed public buildings, urban planning, and a forum to address collective social problems such as crime, poverty, and disease. Antiquity, and particularly texts and artifacts from republican and early imperial Rome, spoke to these needs of a developing city culture. One explanation for the revival of antiquity in thirteenth- and fourteenth-century Italy is that people who lived there recognized certain affinities between their urban world and its problems and the urban world of the ancients.

At the same time, classical literary, philosophical, and artistic culture clearly differed radically both from the chivalric culture of feudalism and from the scholastic culture that flourished in medieval universities. Thus, as the first Italian humanists recognized some affinities between ancient cities and their own communes, they also saw antiquity as a cultural alternative, as a distant, opaque, and in some ways alien society that required skill and effort to understand. This capacity to recognize in antiquity both contextual affinities and stark differences, combined with the desire to study and to emulate its cultural standards, sets Renaissance humanism apart from earlier classical revivals.

The renewed, sustained interest in antiquity that developed within Italian communes took hold first among lawyers, grammarians, and notaries. From the twelfth century on, especially at the University of Bologna, the study of Roman law occupied a central place. Italian lawyers who worked in the urban environment of the communes increasingly turned to Roman legal concepts, Roman methods of analysis, and Roman organizational structures to make sense of the new commercial and social arrangements that were developing around them. Such Roman traditions both conferred legitimacy on novel practices in the communes and seemed to fit a developing urban culture. And, because law was such a prominent discipline within medieval and early modern universities, many humanists studied it and thus came to know antiquity initially through its jurisprudence.

Grammarians and notaries also played a key initial role in renewing interest in ancient literary culture after 1200 C.E. Grammarians taught Latin. Insofar as they used examples from classical literature as teaching material or as standards of correct speech and writing, they introduced students to the language of antiquity. Although notaries, really a class of professionals trained to produce legal and other public documents, worked in many capacities, they also taught Latin grammar and rhetoric. As the demand for primary education grew in central and northern Italy from the late twelfth century on, notaries increasingly turned to teaching, and elementary education moved increasingly into the hands of laypersons (grammarians and notaries) and out of the hands of clerics. It is in this environment of curricular secularization, of expanding urban culture, and of increased demand for basic education that some writers—among them Lovato dei Lovati and Albertino Mussato—started to imitate classical texts (especially poetry) by modeling their own writing on the writing of ancient Latin authors. Their efforts mark the beginning of the revival of antiquity and the emergence of the new ways of reading and writing that define Renaissance humanism.

Petrarch and the Ancients

Francesco Petrarch was born in 1304 in Arezzo. At that time, he was called simply Francesco, son of Eletta Canigiani and her husband, Ser Petracco. Only later did he adopt his father's given name as his surname. Ser Petracco, like his father and grandfather, had been trained as a notary. Ambition and talent took him from the town of Incisa, his family's home, to the vibrant but politically volatile city of Florence. In the late thirteenth century, such a move promised both opportunities and risks. Florence, like most communes, endured endemic struggles among rival family alliances, each of which exiled its enemies when it gained momentary victory. Although Ser Petracco earned a reputation as a skilled notary and a man of literary culture, he eventually found himself caught between two political factions, and the one he supported lost. In 1302, after a trumped-up accusation of corruption, his property was confiscated and he was summarily sentenced to the amputation of a hand, a large fine, and exile. Ser Petracco fled unhurt to Arezzo, where Francesco was born.

Shortly after Petrarch's birth, his mother returned to her father-in-law's home in Incisa. Petrarch spent his early years there and in Padua. In 1312, the family moved to Carpentras (just outside Avignon), where Petrarch began to study Latin with the teacher Convenevole da Prato. From Carpentras, he and his brother Gherardo went on to study law, first at the University of Montpellier and then at the famed University of Bologna. When their father died in 1326, Petrarch and his brother returned to Avignon.

By 1330, financial need required Petrarch to choose a profession. Rather than pursuing law, which he had come to dislike, he decided to become a cleric, and he accepted a post as household chaplain to Cardinal Giovanni Colonna. Colonna and his brother Giacomo would remain close to Petrarch even after he left the cardinal's service, and Petrarch would continue to depend on such relationships, which united friendship and patronage, throughout his career. This position as household chaplain was the first of several ecclesiastical appointments that Petrarch held. Such posts sometimes carried minimal responsibilities and thus left him time for writing and study. Technically, these positions obligated Petrarch to celibacy. He never married, although he did have two children, a son born in 1337 and a daughter born in 1343.

Petrarch's coronation as poet laureate in 1341 ensured his fame and allowed him to represent his literary talent as an important asset to secular and religious rulers. Indeed, because few generally accepted principles existed by which to adjudicate the conflicts that arose from unstable political situations (quickly shifting alliances, factions that rose to prominence and then collapsed, and several different parties— such as the pope, the Holy Roman emperor, powerful families, and rival communes—who claimed jurisdiction over the same territory or the same persons), Petrarch's prestige and eloquence became weapons of diplomacy. Over the course of his life, he persuaded many powerful men—cardinals, dukes, popes, and kings—that reading ancient authors had equipped him to perform all kinds of important diplomatic and political missions. He was a sought-after emissary, counselor, and publicist as well as an admired writer. As early as 1343, Petrarch traveled to the kingdom of Naples on behalf of Clement VI, who served as pope from 1342 to 1352, to request the release of three men held prisoner there following a territorial dispute. Similarly, in 1360, Petrarch represented the Visconti family, who ruled Milan, at the court of the French king. In addition to such diplomatic missions, Petrarch wrote letters, orations, and treatises dedicated to or at the request of the patrons who supported him. One of his last works, a long letter on how to be a good ruler, was composed at the request of Francesco da Carrara, who had, among other things, given Petrarch the property in the town of Arquà where he lived until his death in 1374 (see Map 2).

Although Petrarch never formally worked in a communal government, his activities on behalf of rulers, patrons, and friends periodically involved him in the tumultuous events of his time. For much of his life, he remained personally committed to two political dreams: the relocation of the papal court from Avignon, where it had resided since 1309, to Rome; and peace and unity in Italy. These two abiding desires find frequent expression in Petrarch's writings. As early as the mid-1330s, he wrote a poem in Italian that celebrated the anticipated relocation of Benedict XII, who served as pope from 1334 to 1342, to Rome. In addition, several sonnets in the *Rime sparse* both condemn the worldliness of the papal court and mourn what Petrarch, alluding to the biblical account of the detention of the Jews in Babylon in the sixth century B.C.E., called the "Babylonian Captivity" of the church in Avignon. Decades later, when circumstances once more seemed favorable, Petrarch spent months composing a letter in Latin to Urban V, who served as pope from 1362 to 1370, imploring him to flout the wishes of the French cardinals and to return to Italy. To Petrarch's great joy, Urban V did leave Avignon for Rome in 1367, but by 1370 political turmoil in the Papal States—the territory in central Italy, including Rome, nominally controlled by the pope—forced him to return to Avignon, where the papal court remained until after Petrarch's death.

Petrarch's other great political dream—for a peaceful, unified Italy—also found frequent expression in his writings and was linked to his appreciation for the greatness of ancient Rome. One of his best

Map 2. Petrarch's Italy.

known and most passionate sonnets, poem 128 in the *Rime sparse,* laments the wounds of war afflicting "My Italy" and ends with an agonized plea for peace. Petrarch also appealed occasionally to rulers whom he thought might be capable of uniting Italy and of preventing war between rival Italian territories. He wrote several letters to Charles IV of Bohemia, who served as Holy Roman emperor from 1355 to 1378, arguing, once in the voice of Rome itself, that he should restore to Italy its past greatness and its centrality in the empire.

More significantly, Petrarch's dream led him to support Cola di Rienzo (1313–1354), a charismatic, ambitious, and self-important man whom Petrarch first met when Cola arrived at the papal court in 1343 as the representative of a new governing council in Rome that had taken power after a popular revolt. The two men shared an enthusiasm for antiquity and became friends. When Cola returned to Rome, he began to lay the groundwork for a revolution that aimed both to end the violent feuding of rival noble families and to restore the city to its glorious dominance in Italy. Cola gained followers. In May 1347, his revolution began with the adoption of a new form of government under which Cola was named tribune, an ancient Roman title used under the republic to designate a powerful legislative official and under the empire to designate a set of important powers assumed by the emperor. By claiming it for himself, Cola proclaimed both his own ambition and his desire to revive Roman institutions and Roman power. Soon after assuming this title, Cola, in an extraordinarily bold gesture, reclaimed for the Roman people all their ancient territorial and jurisdictional rights of sovereignty, a claim that tried to deny several centuries of complex political development on three continents.

During the early months of Cola's revolution, Petrarch urged him on and exhorted the Roman people to reclaim their destiny as defenders of liberty and guardians of unity and peace. Even when Cola's egoism and his audacity turned many against him, Petrarch stood by him as the only viable candidate for a huge and arduous task. In the end, however, Cola lost even Petrarch's support. Having fallen both to his own arrogance and to a nobility and papacy that eventually united against him, Cola di Rienzo abdicated in December 1347, just seven months after his revolution had begun.

Although Petrarch's many diplomatic missions, his attacks on the Avignon papacy, and his enthusiasm for Cola di Rienzo attest to his political commitments, he avoided holding political office or devoting himself to the service of a single city. He was instead a restless man. Early in his career, he lived in and around Avignon, and despite his anti-Avignon polemics, he gained much from the vibrant intellectual community that thrived at the papal curia (the offices and staff of the pope) and from the contacts he made there. Later, Petrarch lived in other urban cultural centers. He lived for some years in Milan as a guest of the ruling Visconti family, and he lived briefly in Padua, Parma, and Venice. He also spent much time in the country, in Vaucluse and in Arquà, places that offered peace and a greater opportunity for quiet reflection and study. Wherever he was, and no matter who supported him or employed him, Petrarch found time to read and to write. His collected works—letters, dialogues, treatises, polemics, pastoral poems, sonnets, an epic, biographies, collections of ancient exempla and stories, and critical editions—fill many volumes. When he died, he left many projects unfinished.

After he died, Petrarch was celebrated by one of his followers, Coluccio Salutati (1331–1406), as a writer whose versatility and talent elevated him above even Virgil and Cicero, the towering greats of Latin literature. Salutati's effusive praise gives some indication of just how famous Petrarch had become by the time of his death. And precisely because he had been so sought after and so well-known, Petrarch had been an extraordinarily effective lobbyist for literary education as well as a masterful image creator. His self-presentation and his passionate insistence on the inestimable ethical value of reading ancient texts had convinced many of his contemporaries to support the humanist movement.

Defining Humanism

For Petrarch, the humanist project, now often summarized cavalierly as "the revival of antiquity," was anything but simple. It is therefore very important to understand what *humanism* can mean and what it meant to Petrarch. Among historians of early modern Europe, humanism is often juxtaposed to *scholasticism,* where scholasticism refers in a general way to the methods of inquiry, analysis, and expression that dominated late medieval scholarship and education. In this context, some scholars use humanism to describe an aesthetic that relies on classical examples rather than abstract rules of style. Others use humanism to describe a logical method that was different from the one routinely taught in fourteenth-century universities. Still others use it to refer to a focus on practical ethical questions rather than philosophical speculation, to a curriculum grounded in classical grammar and rhetoric, or to a cultural agenda designed to meet the needs of a rising urban elite. These various definitions, which all understand humanism as a movement to revive aspects of the classical past, attest to the efforts of literally generations of historians to identify precisely what in European culture changed between the fourteenth and seventeenth centuries and to explain how these changes were shaped by artifacts recovered from antiquity.

When, however, *humanism* is used in a philosophical context, its range of meanings is somewhat different. Here it can signify a view of the human person that emphasizes some set of characteristics that all humans supposedly share. Such characteristics might include a capacity for reason, an entitlement to rights, a capacity for language, or free will. Humanism in this context can mean a method of literary interpretation that equates what the author meant to say with the meaning of a text. Or it might mean a belief in the autonomy of the individual to fashion his or her own identity. Finally, humanism in a philosophical context can mean, as it does in the phrase "secular humanism," an analytical framework that focuses on purely human capacities and responsibilities in this world, independent of religion. In these philosophical contexts, humanism refers to a variety of assumptions about subjectivity, human agency, and human cultural production. These assumptions may have emerged in the wake of Renaissance humanism, but they are analytically distinct from it.

Although these two uses of the term are distinct, they are related in important ways. Indeed, in what remains an extraordinarily influential portrait of the Italian Renaissance, Jacob Burckhardt claimed in the late nineteenth century that the rebirth of antiquity was the mechanism through which a new, modern view of the individual found expression. In other words, Burckhardt described a close connection between certain assumptions about the human person and the movement to emulate cultural standards exemplified in classical Latin (and, from the fifteenth century on, Greek) texts. Although much subsequent scholarship has questioned his conclusions, Burckhardt's perspective remains important. From this perspective, one that asserts a connection between a new view of the human person and a movement to revive antiquity, we can see how Renaissance humanists made certain philosophical assumptions even when they scorned conventional philosophical inquiry as dry, uninspiring, and "scholastic."

The humanist movement to revive antiquity had philosophical implications because its aim of emulating a distant culture was based on identifiable assumptions about human nature, time, and historical change. That is, in seeking to recover antiquity, humanists had to believe that the chronological gap separating them from the ancients was bridgeable. They had to believe that very distant texts could speak meaningfully to their contemporaries, that humans living in the fourteenth century had enough in common with the ancients to make reading their works rewarding. However, those who pursued this aim of emulating antiquity did not necessarily adopt a common, single philosophical outlook. Renaissance humanists were a heterogeneous and eclectic group. Therefore, although we can point to certain assumptions that underlie humanism's aims, we cannot define humanism as a particular philosophical method or as a particular school of thought.

Rather, Renaissance humanism can be defined most accurately as a range of textual practices—ways of reading and writing—that bridged the gap between the present and the classical and early Christian past. Petrarch and his successors accepted as ideals for their own time cultural (literary and moral) standards that they found expressed in the works of ancient Roman (and later Greek) authors. They assumed that these authors could, despite their acknowledged distance, speak wisely about modern concerns. The writings of early Renaissance humanists thus imagine a context in which authors ancient and modern, Christian and pagan, can converse in a common language about abiding questions fundamental to the human condition. These questions might revolve around abstract issues, such as the nature and obligations of selfhood, human desire and its satisfaction, friendship and familial relations, or the constitution and preservation of political community. Or they might be concrete, such as how to cure gout, how to deal with an uncooperative servant, or how to set up an efficient household. From this perspective, humanism is best understood not as a philosophy or even as an educational program based on the classics but rather as a set of reading and writing practices (annotation, emendation, citation, and imitation, for example) through which authors like Petrarch sought to make relevant in their own day the writings of other authors long dead.

This desire to make the ancients speak required the humanists to balance contradictory approaches to the classical texts they read. Indeed, the historian Anthony Grafton has suggested that the humanist project of recovery was fundamentally characterized by a kind of "interpretive schizophrenia." On the one hand, humanist scholars, motivated by a deep appreciation for the values of classical civilization, believed that ancient texts had universal significance and could thus serve the needs of the present or of any age. The humanist effort to recover such texts was no empty, antiquarian gesture of preservation for its own sake but a cultural mission of unbounded promise. Once the works of antiquity were restored to their original form, they would stand as timeless monuments to the potential of human intellect and creativity. On the other hand, the arduous training required to interpret, correct, edit, and translate classical sources forced humanist scholars to recognize the enormous chasm that separated their world from that of the ancients. "Classical" texts, however eloquent, spoke to circumstances and experiences very distant from those of their humanist admirers.

Most humanists adopted aspects of each of these personalities—the one romantic and universalizing, the other distancing and historical—yet their "schizophrenia" took innumerable forms. Indeed, the more we study humanism, the more attuned we become to the contradictions and complexities evident in humanist approaches to defining and interpreting antiquity. For these reasons, and in spite of the evident philosophical implications of a movement to revive standards from a long-ago culture, Renaissance humanism is best provisionally defined as the concrete ways of reading and writing through which Petrarch and his successors brought words, texts, styles, and forms from the distant past into the early modern present. As we shall see, *The Secret,* more than any other of Petrarch's works, illustrates these important reading and writing practices.

The range of genres in which Petrarch wrote suggests the depth of his humanist commitment. Indeed, it is the range of his activities, from editing texts to collecting manscripts to reviving styles and genres, that most obviously distinguishes Petrarch from earlier classically minded writers. Although much of his earliest writing was in Italian, from a young age Petrarch exhibited an interest in ancient Latin literature and in Roman culture that lasted throughout his life. This interest deepened after he first traveled to Rome in 1336, and soon thereafter he devoted more of his time to reading classical texts and to aggressively collecting manuscripts that had preserved them. When these manuscripts contained mistakes, he used his knowledge of Latin to correct them. He even reassembled one text, Livy's (59 B.C.E.–17 C.E.) *History of Rome,* from parts of it he found in different manuscripts.

Petrarch also wrote poems in imitation of Virgil and dialogues formally modeled on those of Cicero. He could do this for the same reason that he could reassemble Livy: because he recognized that classical Latin literature followed stylistic conventions, used a vocabulary, and dealt with subjects that were distinctive and different from

Figure 2. Petrarch Writing, with Figures of Cupid and Laura.

This illustration from a late fourteenth-century manuscript of Petrarch's Italian love poems, the *Canzoniere,* shows Petrarch at a desk writing while a Cupid figure (top center) aims an arrow at him. Laura, Petrarch's beloved, is depicted in the outer right margin.

the conventions, vocabulary, and subjects that characterized the writings of his contemporaries. This capacity to recognize both differences across time and distinctive writing styles was the first step toward emulation.

When Petrarch found and read a collection of Cicero's most private letters in a library in Verona in 1345, he recognized how different these colloquial writings were from the formal, rule-governed epistles common in his own day. Cicero wrote as if he were speaking. He used slang. He left out words. He contradicted himself from one sentence to the next. His indecisiveness, anxiety, ambition, and hopes leaped off the page, at first startling and then captivating Petrarch, who, for all his experience with the carefully crafted letters of his own day, had never read anything as powerful as these. He very consciously began to write as Cicero had written, adopting an equally intimate voice in his letters to his own friends. In part because of Petrarch's influence and example, the personal letter became a key genre for the development of Renaissance humanism. Through letters, humanists made contact with one another. They sought missing classical texts, shared information about manuscripts, and requested feedback on their own writing. Indeed, through letter writing, humanists from Petrarch on created an intellectual community with a common language (classical Latin) that could support their efforts to recover and emulate the literature of antiquity.

Figure 3.   Frontispiece for Petrarch's Manuscript of Virgil's Works.

In the late 1330s, Petrarch commissioned this illustration for his favorite copy of Virgil's works from the artist Simone Martini. The illustration shows Virgil lying under a tree composing his poems. Servius, a late antique grammarian whose commentary on Virgil often accompanied the text, stands to the left, lifting the curtain to reveal the meaning of the poet's words. The three other men in the illustration represent the figures about whom Virgil wrote in his major works: a military leader (*Aeneid*), a farmer (*Georgics*), and a shepherd (*Eclogues*). Petrarch wrote three couplets for this illustration. They read (from top to bottom): "Rich Italian soil, you nourish exceptional poets, but this man allowed you to reach the heights of the Greeks"; "Servius uncovering the lofty hidden wisdom of Virgil, so that they may be known to military leaders, shepherds, and farmers"; and (not shown here) "Mantua brought forth Virgil who wrote the following poems, Siena brought forth Simone who with his hand painted the following."

21

For Petrarch, the community created through letter writing included the dead as well as the living. He wrote to Cicero, Seneca, and Livy; to Horace and Virgil; even to Varro (116–27 B.C.E.), a man whose works survived only in fragments and only because they were quoted by other authors. In these letters, Petrarch wrote as Cicero had written, as if he were speaking. He addressed the ancients not just as great writers but as complex personalities, as real people, whose strengths and flaws he knew well. This desire to befriend ancient authors further distinguishes Petrarch from his predecessors, and it suggests how he used his reading and writing to create a language and a set of contexts in which temporal distance was overcome. The dead and the living could converse about issues of abiding concern: the importance of friendship, the nature of virtue, the pain of grief, the inevitability of death. Such encounters had, according to Petrarch, an ethical as well as a literary value. And insofar as humanist practices enabled the ancients to speak across time, those practices had an ethical value as well.

Petrarch had an extraordinary capacity to imagine the past as a place very different from the present. He knew better than most just how different pagan Rome was from his own Christian age. Yet Petrarch also believed that classical authors could, through the efforts of scholars and writers like himself, be made to speak fruitfully to his contemporaries. His desire to recover and to emulate antiquity in no way abrogated his commitment to Christianity. For Petrarch, however, Christianity was not just a system of doctrines and a body of knowledge; it was a way of life. Too many of his university-trained contemporaries, Petrarch thought, had forgotten this. Even when these scholars worked to discover the path to virtue and a good life, their writing would never move any reader to follow it.

As modes of inquiry, the disciplines of theology and philosophy that were taught in fourteenth-century universities aimed to arrive at reasonably certain knowledge by following a logical method that systematically addressed counterarguments and exposed contradictions. Historians call these systematic approaches *scholasticism* because they flourished within schools and universities. Students in these disciplines had developed analytical tools, ways of writing, and a technical vocabulary that suited this aim of systematically discovering and organizing knowledge.

Although historians have long recognized scholasticism as a complex set of rigorous intellectual methods that served its aims effectively, this was not Petrarch's opinion of it. From his point of view, shaped as it was by the aesthetic standards of antiquity, the treatises written by academic theologians and philosophers were incomprehensible, boring, and irrelevant. They dwelt on insignificant questions, ignoring the central question of how humans ought to live. What good is it, Petrarch argued, to know all kinds of trivial facts about the natural world or even about the nature of the angels in heaven if you don't know how to live your own life? And what is the purpose of writing treatises that, even if true, induce not virtuous action but sleep? Petrarch criticized these academics for pursuing useless knowledge through a form of writing that failed to inspire. How different, he thought, were the authors of antiquity, whose oratorical style was meant to move and persuade, to galvanize the will. For us, an analogous comparison might be between a law review article—plodding, thorough, heavily footnoted, relentlessly accurate—and a dramatic, if one-sided, courtroom closing argument. Because Petrarch believed that words should inspire action, he much preferred early Christian literature—the Bible and the works of Augustine and other fourth- and fifth-century writers—to the writings of his scholastic contemporaries. Furthermore, he thought that Christians who read skilled ancient rhetoricians such as Cicero, Virgil, and Seneca, as well as early Christian writers trained in ancient rhetoric, such as Augustine, Ambrose (339–397 C.E.), and Jerome (ca. 342–420 C.E.), were more likely to lead virtuous lives than people who read theological and philosophical works written in his own day.

For Petrarch, then, the recovery of antiquity—or humanism—was not just a literary but an ethical project. Ancient writings could serve the contemporary quest for the good life even though the vast majority of these writings predated, ignored, or condemned Christianity. More than anything else, Petrarch's conviction that the study and emulation of classical authors could enable virtue in a Christian context distinguishes him from his predecessors. *The Secret* illustrates this conviction.

Humanism after Petrarch

Petrarch's immediate followers—Salutati, Guarino of Verona (1374–1460), Leonardo Bruni (ca. 1370–1444), and Lorenzo Valla (1407–1457)—sought to revive and to participate in a broad literary culture that took its standards from antiquity. They thought about and believed in the power of such a culture to ennoble the whole of society.

In their writings, they both advocated broad educational reform and sought to sustain a community in which classical studies could flourish not as an end in itself but because, they argued, such studies produced human beings better able to lead good, virtuous lives.

The activities of the early humanists reflected these aims. They sought out, corrected, and copied manuscripts of classical Latin texts so that these would be more widely available. Some translated Greek texts. They wrote grammatical handbooks and manuals of style; they elucidated the rhetorical principles of Cicero and Quintilian (ca. 35–100 C.E.); and they imitated classical authors in their own poetry, letters, dialogues, and histories. Through such activities, these men hoped in some sense to partake of and to revive the literary culture and community that they imagined had existed in ancient Rome. For these early humanists, the "scholarly" aspects of the revival of antiquity could not be separated from a more fundamental cultural mission. In their writing, the recovery of classical texts is necessarily bound up with claims about the redemptive power of reading, the timelessness of ancient norms, and what it means to be human.

Such claims led Petrarch's successors to advocate making the study and imitation of ancient literary texts foundational to a "good" education. Indeed, they argued that such studies (which only they could teach) best prepared young men to lead virtuous, productive lives. Their arguments proved persuasive, and some humanist teachers—Pier Paolo Vergerio (1370–1444), Guarino, and Vittorino da Feltre (ca. 1378–1446)—achieved great fame. By the early fifteenth century, more and more powerful families were securing humanist training for their children. At the same time, communal governments, ruling families, and the Catholic Church sought out humanistically trained officials whose rhetorical skills and historical knowledge made them eloquent, persuasive spokesmen both at home and with external powers. Florence in particular employed several distinguished humanists—including Salutati, Bruni, and Poggio Bracciolini (1380–1459)—in the important position of chancellor of the republic.

Once humanistic education became popular among Italian urban elites, the aesthetic and ethical ideals of ancient culture exerted an increasingly powerful impact on civic and political life. This trend is discernible in many cities—Milan, Ferrara, and Padua, for example—and at the papal curia (the offices of the pope), which employed some of the most renowned humanists of the fifteenth century, including Valla. The entanglement of humanism with politics emerged most clearly in Florence, where officials such as Salutati and Bruni used their rhetorical training and their knowledge of the ancient world to craft distinctive, secular interpretations of Italian history that eloquently (if one-sidedly) justified Florentine policies. Yet humanists working in other milieus also used their knowledge in the service of their patrons. Just as Salutati and Bruni relied on classical models to celebrate the virtues of republican Florence and its role as heir to Rome, so humanists who worked for the Visconti family in Milan found classical models that glorified the reign of the emperor Augustus (27 B.C.E.–14 C.E.) and therefore advocated princely rule. In Rome, humanists at the papal curia used their knowledge of antiquity to develop a different interpretation of history—one that emphasized the continuity between classical culture and Christianity. Such examples show how humanists could adapt their training to the needs of their particular employers and patrons.

As humanism and politics became more closely entangled, the civic pride that had accompanied the development of the Italian communes increasingly found expression in artistic projects inspired by artifacts from antiquity. The chapels and palaces that Filippo Brunelleschi (1377–1446) designed for Florentine families, Donatello's (1386–1466) statues in the Orsanmichele (Oratory of Saint Michael), donated by the guild of gun manufacturers, and the frescoes of Masaccio (1401–1428) that were commissioned by the Brancacci family for the Church of Santa Maria del Carmine all attest to the appeal of ancient aesthetic ideals among the Florentine elite. Soon humanists and artists developed more confidence in their ability to emulate and even to surpass their classical models. The humanist Leon Battista Alberti (1404–1472) praised Brunelleschi's design for the dome of Florence's main cathedral as an unprecedented feat of engineering. Over time, other Italian cities and, most important, the papacy became important patrons of art inspired by antiquity.

By the mid-fifteenth century, humanism had become established, and its practitioners enjoyed the support of social institutions and the patronage of those in power. Many humanists could thus take for granted the value of what they did. Furthermore, the efforts of earlier generations made it possible for their followers to acquire quickly and with relative ease a basic fluency in classical literary culture. This alone no longer seemed a heroic feat. Consequently, humanism after the mid-fifteenth century took what we might call a scholarly turn. Increasingly, men such as Domizio Calderini (ca. 1447–1478) and Niccolò Perotti (1429–1480) focused primarily on the technical dimensions of recovering the past. They ceased to emphasize the transformative powers of classical culture and concentrated instead on the technical challenge of restoring each ancient text to its original form.

The practices of these later humanists attest to their shift in focus. If earlier generations had concentrated on ancient authors worthy of emulation, these humanists sought out the most impenetrable, least imitable examples of classical Latin writing. If earlier humanists wrote letters, orations, and histories, their more scholarly successors wrote line-by-line commentaries and annotations to accompany particularly unyielding texts. In short, over the course of the Renaissance, technical, more narrowly focused terms and practices came to replace broader literary ones in humanist discourse.

This does not mean, however, that the broader claims of humanism have disappeared. Indeed, the educational ideals that humanism proclaimed continued to shape curricula in the West for centuries and still shape debates about the aims of education and the relationship between education and citizenship. Furthermore, several of the assumptions underlying the recovery and emulation of antiquity continue to inform modern understandings of textual interpretation, of the relationship of the present to the past, and, ultimately, of what it means to be human. We are, in this sense, Petrarch's heirs.

THE SECRET

A Humanist Manifesto

Although it was written at the dawn of the revival of antiquity in fourteenth-century Italy, *The Secret* illustrates more clearly than many later writings several key ideas and practices that underlay the Renaissance humanist movement and, more generally, that ground the humanist tradition and sustain its legacy. In particular, *The Secret* imitates an ancient genre, revives a classical approach to ethics, and argues for the redemptive power of reading.

In a gesture characteristic of the Renaissance humanist movement, *The Secret* resurrects a classical genre, the dialogue, by explicitly mimicking Plato and Cicero. Of course, late antique and medieval writers had composed dialogues, and those of Augustine and Boethius (ca. 480–524 C.E.) clearly influenced Petrarch. Like *The Secret,* Augustine's *The Teacher* and Boethius's *Consolation of Philosophy* record a conversation between a kind of a teacher and a student or follower and emphasize reading as a central activity in the quest for the highest good. However, in these earlier dialogues, one interlocutor, the teacher figure, eventually dominates, and his tone grows progressively more abstract and timeless; the dialogue becomes a monologue, very similar to a philosophical treatise. In contrast, the classical, and especially the Ciceronian, dialogue presents more than one perspective on a given question, leaving some freedom to the reader to choose. Furthermore, the classical dialogue situates speakers in a specific time and place and also respects differences in voice: Different speakers represent different positions. Individual personalities speak, argue, and compare their positions, making the dialogue less abstract and better able to connect general ethical questions (What is virtue?) to concrete human experience (How should my son choose his wife?). For humanists, making these connections was a central task of moral philosophy, a task, they claimed, that much medieval writing had ignored but that many classical texts exemplified. By imitating the dialogue in its classical form, Petrarch and his fifteenth-century successors were able to forge a new way of talking about ethics that survived as a part of the humanist tradition long after the dialogue as a genre declined in importance in the sixteenth century.

In addition to reviving an important classical genre, which in turn facilitated a new way of talking about ethics, *The Secret* also lays out ideas and assumptions that became central components of the humanist tradition. These components include ideas about the value of literature and the right way to read it, approaches to interpreting the past and connecting it to the present, and assumptions about what it means to be human. Aspects of all these ideas and assumptions endure today.

First, *The Secret* insists on the redemptive power of ancient literature. That is, it shows how reading Cicero, Virgil, Seneca, and other authors in the right way can enable the human search for happiness and spiritual well-being. In Petrarch's day, this argument countered claims, mostly from clerics, that ancient literature was pagan literature and therefore not useful for those who sought to lead virtuous Christian lives. In our own day, arguments about the redemptive power of a given canon of literature underlie both conservative claims about high school and college curricula, in particular about the foundational importance of Western civilization courses, and liberal arguments about the relevance of study in the humanities in modern, technology-driven societies. Both kinds of arguments assert that reading is morally efficacious and that books can save us.

Second, *The Secret* argues that readers who want to tap the redemptive power of ancient literature should adopt certain strategies of interpretation and above all should learn to identify with what they read so that they understand their own experience in the terms of ancient texts. In other words, *The Secret* offers this advice: Use ancient texts to express and define your own life. Analyze your awareness of death in the words of Virgil (66–67). Express your intellectual conviction in the language of Seneca (136), your uncertainty with a line from Horace (139), and your resolve in the words of Cicero (105). Take your definition of desire from Ovid (57). If you find yourself surrendering to vanity, repeat the advice that Seneca gave to his student Lucilius (76). Juvenal can expose your greed (78–79). By arguing for this kind of reading, *The Secret* also is arguing for the ongoing relevance of the ancient Greek and Roman past, as well as for a particular way of connecting modern persons to that past. Even though Cicero and Virgil lived in a distant time and a different culture, their works remain relevant because their words can best capture the experiences of subsequent generations. By understanding ourselves in their terms, we internalize and perpetuate the values that they represent. During the early modern period, this argument justified the humanist project of recovering and emulating antiquity by holding up ancient texts as true and timeless records of human experience that could speak to all. In our own day, arguments that privilege reading through identification can sustain our sense of connectedness to the past and validate values that we inherit.

Finally, as *The Secret* makes these claims about the redemptive power of ancient literature (read in the right way), it also makes assumptions about the creature being redeemed and thus assumptions about what it means to be human. Because Petrarch's dialogue implies that the words of dead and distant authors can describe the experiences of modern people, the text assumes that something about the human experience or human nature remains the same through time. All humans, no matter when or where they live, share some capacities and attributes. In Petrarch's day, this assumption allowed him and his successors to imagine a community in which dead and living authors could "converse" about issues of abiding human concern. It allowed him to view Cicero, Livy, Seneca, and Virgil as his friends. Petrarch expressed exactly this sentiment in a letter, written in 1353, that describes his life in Vaucluse:

> I often bring together from all places and every age all the friends I have or have had, not only those known through face-to-face contact and who have lived during my lifetime, but also those who died many centuries before me, those known to me only through the mediation of writing, those whose actions and mind, or character

and life, or eloquence and intellect I admire. And I more eagerly live among these friends than with my contemporaries who imagine themselves alive whenever they, exhaling I do not know what kind of rank stuff, see a hint of their own breath in the cold air. (*Familiar Letters,* XV, 3, 14)

For Petrarch, the assumption of a shared humanness made possible friendships that spanned a millennium. In our own day, this assumption grounds general ethical claims that, in the name of human rights, transcend the attributes of gender, ethnicity, religion, race, and nationality that differentiate people.

These ideas about the redemptive power of literature, about how to read in the right way, and about what it means to be human form an important part of the humanist legacy that we inherit from Petrarch. They suggest how Petrarch's efforts to revive antiquity relate to much later historical developments and especially to the rise of the concept of human rights. We turn now to how these ideas are expressed and function in *The Secret.*

The Composition and Structure of *The Secret*

The Secret is composed of three dialogues between two interlocutors (speakers): Franciscus, a fictionalized version of Petrarch, and Augustinus, a fictionalized version of Augustine, a key figure in the development of Christian thought in the fourth and fifth centuries. These conversations, in which Augustinus aims to cure Franciscus of the diseases afflicting his soul, take place in the presence of Truth, who appears in human form. One day, the prologue states, as Franciscus is reflecting on the course of his life, a woman suddenly appears before him. The woman is so dazzlingly beautiful that he can scarcely look at her without averting his eyes. This woman, he learns, is Truth. Truth has seen how miserable Franciscus is, and she has asked Augustinus, a man who himself endured painful spiritual struggles and whom Franciscus knows and respects, to intercede. Over the next three days, the two men talk intimately about Franciscus's unhappiness. After the discussion ends, Franciscus decides to write down what was said so that by reading it, he can relive the pleasure he derived from the original conversations. At the same time, he resolves to keep the book private, and he calls it *The Secret.*

In each of the conversations, Augustinus explores different aspects of Franciscus's spiritual condition. The first book primarily addresses the role of the human will in perpetuating human unhappiness. The second analyzes how Franciscus is afflicted by the specific sins of pride, envy, greed, gluttony, anger, lust, and apathy. A monastic tradition dating back to the sixth century identifies these sins as cardinal, or deadly, because they easily give rise to other sins. The third book probes the two most formidable obstacles to Franciscus's spiritual well-being: his desire for the mortal woman Laura, which interferes with his love for God, and his quest for earthly fame as a writer, which distracts him from the care of his soul.

The Secret is a complex text that can support many different, even conflicting, interpretations. Almost every aspect of it, from when it was written to what it means, has given rise to heated debates among readers. The following questions recur in these debates: Does *The Secret* reflect specific events in Petrarch's life or a specific stage in his intellectual development? If Augustinus is based on the historical Augustine, why doesn't he quote himself and other Christian authors more frequently? Why is the end of the dialogue so ambivalent? Does Franciscus take Augustinus's advice, or doesn't he? How does this lack of a resolute ending shape interpretations of the dialogue as a whole?

Although scholars do not agree even on how to approach these questions, most generally accept that Petrarch drafted *The Secret* in 1347 and revised it, more or less extensively, until 1353. Petrarch often revised or rewrote his works. When he collected and organized his personal letters for publication, he rewrote several of them, and he even composed new letters and backdated them to fill in the gaps in his correspondence. Letters he dates in the 1330s were really produced in the 1350s. Indeed, Petrarch's most famous letter, about his climb up Mont Ventoux, is dated 1336 but was actually written in 1353, after its addressee was already dead. Such a method of composition— drafting, reordering, rewriting, and inventing—makes precise dating very difficult and also undermines the usefulness of Petrarch's individual writings for reconstructing the chronology of his intellectual life. Even if *The Secret* does refer to a specific time of spiritual crisis (a dubious claim), we cannot with any certainty identify when it was. Thus readers have in general abandoned a strict autobiographical approach to *The Secret* and focused more on the question of what it might mean.

This question is even harder to approach. First, who are the interlocutors? Augustinus, though clearly based on Augustine, espouses ideas that are completely at odds with those expressed in Augustine's writings. For example, in *The Secret* Augustinus describes his conversion as an act of human will, whereas Augustine's *Confessions* highlight the role of divine grace. Furthermore, Petrarch's Augustinus almost never quotes Augustine. Indeed, he prefers classical pagan authors to Christian ones. This dissonance between the historical Augustine and Petrarch's Augustinus has led readers to ascribe less literal identities to the two speakers in *The Secret*. Augustinus might represent Petrarch's Christian conscience, with Franciscus speaking for his literary aspirations. Or perhaps Augustinus is the man Petrarch wanted to become, and Franciscus is his current self. This introduction proposes that Petrarch created in Augustinus a version of Augustine who defines humanist reading practices as redemptive.

Augustinus

The historical Augustine was a central figure in the consolidation of Christian doctrine during the late fourth century. Born in Tagaste (now Souk Ahras, Algeria), in what was then Numidia, he converted to Christianity under the influence of Ambrose of Milan, another towering figure in the fourth-century Catholic Church. From 396 to 430, Augustine was bishop of Hippo (now Annaba, Algeria), in Roman North Africa (see Map 3). From this position, Augustine spoke out on virtually every important religious issue of the day. He wrote treatises about the Trinity and human free will. He wrote commentaries on Genesis and the Psalms. He delivered innumerable sermons in limpid Latin that introduced his North African audiences, whose first language was often Punic, to Christian ideas. And he fiercely combated all non-Catholic religious practices and beliefs—including those of non-Catholic Christians—in a series of scathing (and often utterly misleading) polemics. When he took on traditional Roman religious practices, which he lumped together as "paganism," in *The City of God*, he made the whole of the Roman past, from the founding of the city (eighth century B.C.E.) to its recent invasion (410 C.E.) by the Visigoth Alaric, fade away in the blaze of a greater Christian glory. All of these writings, and others too numerous to name, exerted an enormous impact on the development of Catholic Christian teaching and practice.

No one would dispute Augustine's importance for Christian history, yet this alone does not account for his appearance as a speaker in *The Secret*. Why did Petrarch choose to write an imaginary conversation between a fictionalized representation of himself and a fictionalized representation of a fourth-century church father? Why did he choose Augustine? The most obvious answer is that Petrarch loved Augustine's

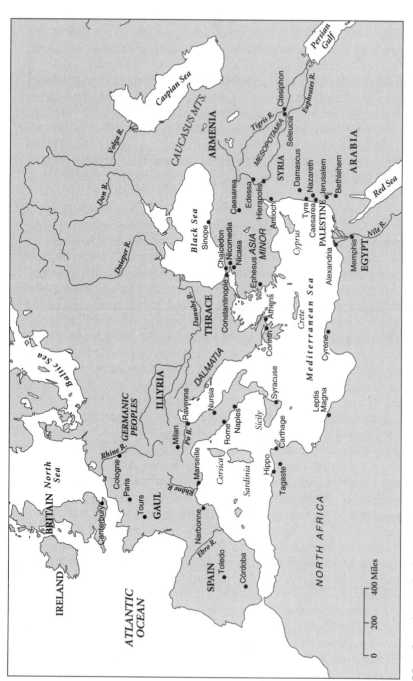

Map 3. Augustine's Mediterranean.

works and counted the saint among his favorite authors. Indeed, one of his earliest known book purchases, made in 1325, was of *The City of God,* and he continued to collect and to annotate manuscripts containing Augustine's works throughout his life. His favorite of Augustine's writings, and perhaps the reason he used Augustinus as an interlocutor in his own autobiographical text, *The Secret,* was the *Confessions.* Written between 397 and 400, the *Confessions* recount the intellectual and spiritual journey that led to Augustine's acceptance, at the age of thirty-one, of the truth of Catholic Christianity. This was not an easy trip. As a young man, Augustine grappled with everything from profound intellectual questions (If God is good, where does evil come from? How can anyone actually believe in the resurrection of the body?), to interpretive puzzles (Why is the Bible so contradictory? Why is its language so unpolished?), to personal crises triggered by a keen awareness of the chasm separating himself as he was from the person he ought to be. Such personal struggles resonated powerfully with Petrarch, who also fought against the distractions of this world. *The Secret* even suggests that Augustine's description of his inner struggles could describe Petrarch's experiences as well.

Augustine's *Confessions* spoke to Petrarch both because of the experiences they recount and because of the way they are written. The *Confessions* link Augustine's spiritual progress very specifically to reading. They recount how Cicero's words convinced Augustine to love virtue, how Platonist writings taught him to think abstractly, and how the apostle Paul's letters moved him to convert. Furthermore, Augustine weaves quotations from these central texts (especially the Psalms) into the story of his life. The *Confessions* thus provided Petrarch, a man who passionately believed in the transformative power of literary activity, with a model of a life story in which reading is depicted as redemptive.

The *Confessions* exerted such a powerful impact on Petrarch that he used its account of Augustine's conversion as a literary model for one of his most famous writings. In this writing, a letter, Petrarch uses an account, probably fictional, of a climb up Mont Ventoux as a way of exploring his spiritual ascent to the good life. Clearly, Petrarch felt a deep affinity with Augustine the sinner, who had refashioned himself according to the discipline of Christianity. When Petrarch decided to write a dialogue about his own spiritual conflicts, he perhaps naturally turned to the author of the *Confessions* as a potential interlocutor.

As a centrally important Christian figure, Augustine was clearly an apt choice for spiritual counselor. Even more significant for Petrarch, however, was the fact that Augustine was steeped in the literature of the ancient world. He lived just after Christianity had become the privileged religion of the Roman Empire. At this time, even as the Catholic Church was both standardizing its theology and consolidating its earthly power, classical texts—the very writings that, a thousand years later, Petrarch would seek to emulate—remained the basis for schooling and literary culture. Because Augustine had planned a career in rhetoric before his conversion, he had absorbed Virgil, Cicero, and other Latin authors so thoroughly that their writing informed his own. As a bishop, he used his classical rhetorical training and familiarity with the Latin literary tradition to craft his sermons, commentaries, letters, and treatises. Thus Augustine's works both express his profound Christian convictions and reflect his intimate familiarity with the works of Cicero and Virgil and other non-Christian writers. His writings suggest, sometimes in spite of his intentions, how pagan literature could serve the aims of a Christian culture. Although Petrarch took this idea much further, Augustine's works helped him to imagine how the (pagan) literature he loved could be made to serve in a (Christian) quest for happiness, spiritual health, and salvation.

Augustinus and Franciscus

Throughout the dialogue, Augustinus proposes various remedies to help Franciscus arrive at spiritual health. Some of these remedies are visual. For example, Augustinus states that if Franciscus is to be cured, he must truly desire to get better. This requires Franciscus to confront his own mortality by attending the funerals of friends or by watching as bodies are prepared for burial. Augustinus suggests that the vivid memories of these appalling sights will remind Franciscus that he too will certainly die.

While some of Augustinus's recommendations urge Franciscus to seek out particularly graphic, memorable scenes, most of his suggestions involve ancient texts. He frequently complains that if Franciscus had only appreciated what he had already read, he would have long ago begun to recover. Throughout *The Secret,* Augustinus describes several ways of reading that could serve the quest for spiritual health. The most explicit example of this occurs near the end of the second conversation, where Augustinus advises Franciscus to note the passages that have the power to move his soul and to study those passages until they become a part of him, so that whenever he feels distracted from or confused about the quest for true health, he can remember and find strength in the words he has absorbed.

In this passage, Augustinus points to some very important and distinctive features of humanist reading, which presumes that ancient texts express universal truths with which all readers can identify and from which all readers can benefit. Because these texts are timeless, each reader will find in them principles by which to live and even descriptions of his or her own experiences. This assumption about the universal value of ancient literature justifies its recovery and emulation. The texts most likely to provide worthy insights to all people at all times are those from ancient Greece and Rome.

Although this passage perhaps offers the most explicit justification in *The Secret* for a central humanist reading practice, Augustinus and Franciscus also discuss and even demonstrate other important humanist ways of reading and strategies of interpretation. Indeed, the entire dialogue is structured around quotations from classical texts that the two speakers first cite and then discuss. Taken together, these discussions attest both to the centrality of reading in the humanist project of recovering antiquity and to the variety of ways of reading that humanists practiced. On what assumptions are these reading practices based? How, according to *The Secret,* do these practices serve the quest for human happiness and even salvation?

Because Augustinus is based on a famous Christian saint, we might expect him to refer frequently to Christian texts and especially to the Bible. In other words, we might expect him to express a consistently Christian view of human happiness and spiritual health using evidence from the Bible and other authoritative Christian writings, as the historical Augustine did in the *Confessions*. This expectation heightens when, near the beginning of the first book of the dialogue, both interlocutors mention the *Confessions,* suggesting that the story told there could be Franciscus's own and that he, like the historical Augustine, will move, by way of a conversion experience triggered by a biblical text, from a state of conflict and inner turmoil to happiness and peace. Furthermore, biblical texts, especially the Psalms, play a central role in the structure of the *Confessions*. If *The Secret* is to tell a story analogous to the one told in the *Confessions,* we would expect an interlocutor named Augustinus to base his claims on authoritative Christian sources.

This is not, however, what Augustinus does. Indeed, throughout the dialogue, classical pagan literature provides much of the language in which the conversations are conducted, the language in which Franciscus describes his unhappiness and Augustinus offers his diagnosis and cure. Both speakers constantly refer to and quote the writings of Cicero, Virgil, Seneca, Horace, and other Roman (and pagan) authors and rarely refer to specifically Christian texts.

For example, throughout much of the first book, Augustinus tries to persuade Franciscus that Franciscus has never truly desired happiness. Augustinus makes this case in classical quotations. First, he uses the words of classical authors to describe Franciscus's condition: I could say of you, Augustinus writes, what Virgil wrote in the *Aeneid:* "The mind remains unmoved, fruitless tears pour down" (page 56 in this volume). Second, Augustinus takes definitions of key terms from classical texts, as when he quotes Ovid's definition of desire: "To want is not enough; if you are to possess something, it is necessary that you long for it" (page 57). Even when, near the beginning of this first book, Augustinus begins to define what happiness is and how to find it, he relies not on Christian sources but on Cicero and Virgil. Cicero, Augustinus states, has demonstrated that virtue and happiness go together (pages 51–52). Virgil warns that the path to both is open to a very few (page 52). That an interlocutor modeled on a Christian saint relies so heavily on classical literature poses an interpretive challenge to readers of *The Secret:* Why does Petrarch create a figure named Augustinus who speaks through the words of pagan poets in a dialogue about spiritual health?

Laura

In *The Secret,* Augustinus aims to "cure" Franciscus—that is, to equip Franciscus to devote himself single-mindedly to higher, spiritual things. This kind of devotion is difficult for humans to sustain because while on earth, humans exist in a material body and therefore are easily distracted by the sights, sounds, and objects they perceive around them, as well as by their bodily desires for food, drink, sleep, and sex. Thus one step on the path to virtue and happiness, as Augustinus defines these, is the liberation of the soul, wherein resides the true, abiding essence of the human person, from the corrupting influences of the body or flesh. Early on in the dialogue, Augustinus uses quotations from Virgil's *Aeneid* and from the Bible to describe the dichotomy between the human body and soul. This description holds the senses entirely responsible for the derangement of the purer soul:

Do not doubt that your soul, although it originated in heaven, has degenerated significantly from its original nobility because of the contamination caused by contact with the body in which it is enclosed. Indeed, the soul has not only degenerated, it has, after so much time, become numb. It has been made to forget its own origin and supernatural maker. (page 68)

Such a view of the human person both makes the body incidental to our "real" selves—our disembodied souls—and implicates the mere functioning of the bodily senses in our fall from grace. To achieve virtue, then, is to abandon the specificity of embodiment, an act that frees humans from the corrupting pull of the flesh. Abandoning the body also enables distinctively human bonds among differently located but like-minded individuals (for example, that between Augustinus and Franciscus), among ancients and moderns, among Christians and pagans, to form.

As the conversation proceeds, Augustinus tries to persuade Franciscus that he must somehow detach himself from his body and that this means he must give up his (unconsummated) love for the mortal woman Laura, which is derailing his progress and diluting his love for God. Laura, a woman whose identity and historicity remain debated today, was Petrarch's (possibly imaginary) muse. According to Petrarch, he first saw her in 1327 in the Church of Saint Clare in Avignon, and from then on he was devoted to her. Whether imaginary, fictionalized, or historical, Laura remained his distant love and a source of poetic inspiration for him throughout his life. His most famous Italian poem collection, *Rime sparse,* often called the *canzoniere,* tells of her powerful effect on him, how from the first moment he saw her, he has longed only to describe her beauty and to allow her virtue to lead him to God. As Petrarch details the passionate feelings that Laura evokes in him, he exposes the complexities of his own desires. He wants to write about her shining eyes as lights illuminating his path to heaven, yet the very act of describing their beauty awakes in him a desire that is sensual and physical. In some sense, then, these poems about Laura explore the interrelationships between the desires of the soul and the desires of the body. In so doing, they reveal the futility, and in fact the high cost, of imagining that these desires can ever be definitively separated.

In *The Secret,* however, Augustinus insists that any kind of love for a mortal woman can only be destructive because it is inevitably and fundamentally physical. Although Franciscus concedes many of

Augustinus's claims, he vehemently disputes this characterization of his feelings for Laura as mere lust. Rather, Franciscus claims that he loves her soul. Moreover, it is Laura and the example of her devotion that have moved him to devote himself to higher things. Laura, Franciscus insists, is not of this world. Her passion burns only for heaven. Far from a distraction, she is his inspiration.

Augustinus scoffs at this claim. Are you telling me, he asks, that if she were hideously ugly, you would still devote yourself to her? It is her physical beauty that captivates you and makes you want her. You have become dependent on a mortal woman, Augustinus argues, who is nothing but a body that will age and rot, and you do not even see how this puerile infatuation distracts your soul from higher things and happiness. That is, even as Franciscus maintains that it was precisely Laura's soul and particularly her yearning for the divine that made him long for a cure, Augustinus relentlessly binds Laura to the earth, confines her to the transient body, and uses her to symbolize the corrupt pull of the flesh and the inevitable decay of death. This increasingly close association of Laura, a woman, with the body raises important interpretive questions for modern readers of *The Secret*. Within the terms given by Petrarch and his successors, can women seek virtue and happiness? Can women be humanists? *The Secret* leaves these questions unanswered.

Franciscus

Just as, in order to be cured, Franciscus must abandon his love for Laura, so he must also give up the heroically ambitious writing projects he has taken on to achieve lasting glory. As Augustinus tries, with rising exasperation, to persuade Franciscus of this, he relies on classical quotations, as he has throughout the dialogue. However, Franciscus begins to resist this approach, questioning whether the passages from Cicero and Virgil that Augustinus cites actually apply to his situation. Augustinus continues to prescribe a cure that centers on rightly interpreting and using the books of others, but can these texts always speak "truly" to Franciscus's experience?

Perhaps for this reason, as Augustinus discusses the final problem addressed in the dialogue, the problem of literary ambition, he relies more frequently on passages from the writings of Franciscus—that is, of Petrarch. "I warn you using your own words" (page 125), states Augustinus as he cites a line from one of Petrarch's Latin poems. Similarly, when he describes the demands of fame, Augustinus uses words from Petrarch's Latin poem *Africa:* "If in your poem *Africa* you make the fiercest of enemies offer this advice to your Scipio, then allow this pious father to offer the same counsel to you" (page 131). Augustinus continues to rely on *Africa* as he gives his own judgment on fame: "Do you recognize this verse? You wrote it" (page 143). This way, as Augustinus suggests, Franciscus's spiritual illness will be conquered by his own words. Franciscus, however, continues to resist.

Augustinus's use of Petrarch's writing here elevates Petrarch, an author, to a status equal to the other authors—Cicero, Seneca, Virgil, Horace—upon whom Augustinus relies. His works, too, can bring redemption. Thus Petrarch, the father of humanism, proclaims the legitimacy of his own authorial voice as one within a long and venerable tradition, a continuing conversation whose terms transcend historical circumstance and whose participants, by their participation, transgress the bounds of mortality. The *Secret* creates a literary context in which authors ancient and modern confront one another as equals in the pages of Latin texts.

And yet it is precisely authorship, the act of writing, that Augustinus castigates at the end of the dialogues when he urges Franciscus to abandon his own literary projects:

> Lay down the great burdens of history. The deeds of the Romans have been sufficiently depicted both by their own reputation and through the ingenuity of others. Abandon Africa and leave it to its possessors, for there you will acquire no glory, either for Scipio or for yourself. Scipio could not be extolled more highly than he already is, and you are only struggling behind him on an indirect path.
>
> Once these things have been put in their place, then finally return yourself to yourself and, to come back to the main point of our discussion, begin to think about death, which you slowly and unknowingly are approaching. (page 144)

How can this be? If reading literature can, as the structure of *The Secret* argues, bring redemption, why does Augustinus urge Franciscus to abandon his own literary projects? If *Africa,* like the poems of Virgil and the dialogues of Cicero, can serve in the human quest for self-understanding and spiritual fulfillment (as Augustinus's use of it suggests), why does Augustinus urge Franciscus to give it up? How can the conclusion of the dialogue condemn those very activities—reading and writing—that have made the encounter between these two interlocutors both possible and profitable?

The irresolute conclusion of *The Secret* may express Petrarch's ambivalence about the kind of reading demanded by Augustinus—

that is, reading through identification with and imitation of exemplary texts. This kind of reading risks the falsification of individual experience by understanding it through the words of someone else. Yet this irresolute conclusion also calls into question the very activities of reading and writing that have occupied Franciscus and Augustinus during the dialogue. The structure of *The Secret* assumes that reading and imitating ancient texts enables the quest for human happiness. However, at the end of the dialogue, Augustinus suggests that the activity of writing is precisely what distracts Franciscus from the care of his soul. As such, it is an activity that must be abandoned if he is to pursue happiness with single-minded devotion. By describing writing in this way, Augustinus questions the rationale for the humanist project of recovery and revival. Can distant, dead authors actually speak to the experiences of persons living a millennium later? If we cannot be made better by reading and imitating the ancients, why should we recover them at all? Because *The Secret* raises but does not answer these questions, we are left to struggle with them for ourselves.

The Legacy of *The Secret*

In *The Secret,* Petrarch creates a version of Augustine, one of the most important Christian writers ever, who could authorize humanist practices as redemptive. Throughout the dialogue, Augustinus tries to cure Franciscus by transforming him into a person able to be made better by reading and imitating ancient (and often pagan) texts. From this perspective, Petrarch's dialogue is a humanist manifesto. At the same time, however, the ambivalent ending of *The Secret* implicitly questions all of the assumptions that make humanism imaginable, including the fundamental assumptions that the past is relevant to the present and that reading ancient authors can make people more virtuous. By highlighting, authorizing, and questioning humanism all at the same time, Petrarch's work dramatizes the complexities of this movement that tried to bridge vast cultural and temporal differences by identifying characteristics, concerns, and feelings that men from all times share. Bridging cultural differences in this way, *The Secret* shows us, has costs. Franciscus has to separate his intellect from his body; he has to use the words of others to describe himself; he has to accept that others will use his words in this way. Most significantly, the same conversation that allows Franciscus to aspire to virtue through reading effectively excludes Laura, and through her all women, from the humanist community. We still grapple today with the kind of exclusion that the discussion of Laura enacts in *The Secret*. From this perspective, the questions raised by Petrarch's dialogue, questions about the potential power of reading, about the accessibility and relevance of the dead, about the path to happiness, and about who counts as human—still resonate with us. One would expect nothing less from a humanist text.

A NOTE ON THE TRANSLATION

This version of *The Secret* follows the 1911 translation of William Draper. In revising and updating Draper's translation, I have used the Latin text edited by Enrico Carrara in Francesco Petrarca, *Prose,* ed. G. Martellotti (Milan, 1955). I have also consulted *Opere latine di Francesco Petrarca,* ed. A. Bufano (Turin, 1975), and Francesco Petrarca, *Secretum,* ed. U. Dotti (Rome, 1993). These editions contain Italian translations from which I have learned much. Finally, I have consulted the only other modern English translation, which is out of print: *Petrarch's Secretum, with Introduction, Notes, and Critical Anthology,* trans. and ed. Davy A. Carozza and H. James Shey (New York, 1989). All of these editions and translations contain notes that have guided my reading and pointed me to the sources of Petrarch's quotations and allusions. Without the prior work of these scholars, and particularly of Enrico Carrara, I could not have produced this version of the text.

As I updated Draper's text, I kept three tasks in mind. First, I corrected clear errors in the text, which sometimes assigns passages to the wrong interlocutor or renders a sentence in a way that is at odds with my reading of the Latin and with other modern language translations. Second, I added notes that identify the sources of quotations, explain unclear references (to ancient authors, mythological figures, or Roman history), and that generally make it possible for students to follow and to evaluate the arguments that Franciscus and Augustinus make. Finally, I aimed to render the sense of Petrarch's Latin in readable, modern, accessible English. For example, where Draper renders the Latin *"An non te mortalem esse meministi?"* as "Remember you not you are mortal?" I instead say, "Don't you remember that you are mortal?" (page 49). I generally eliminated expressions that now sound very formal or quaint, such as "give you pardon," "raiment," "I pray you," "Jesu, by Thy mercy," "if it so please you," and "you perceive not," where other, less stilted English could more effectively communicate the meaning of the Latin. Where I have retained a more formal English style, as in parts of the prologue, it signals that Petrarch's Latin is also more formal or more elaborately structured. Likewise, when Franciscus and Augustinus seem to me to be speaking more familiarly, I have used colloquial expressions and phrases in an attempt to communicate the drama and passion of their exchanges. I have done this not to transform Petrarch into a writer of modern

English but rather to allow his modern readers to discover the abiding significance of his thought.

For these same reasons of accessibility and readability, I have added words to clarify ambiguous or elliptical passages. For example, I have translated *"voluntatem impotentiam vocas"* (literally, "you call inability will") as "what you call inability is really a question of will" (page 148). Similarly, because the persuasive power of some of the longer speeches stems in part from the contrast between shorter, simple declarations and the more elaborate constructions that elucidate them, I have sometimes repeated key words (prepositions, subject pronouns, conjunctions) in English that are not repeated in the Latin to convey the length and rhythm of the original sentences. I also have added words when I thought it necessary to convey the impact and the meaning of the original. When Augustinus begins, in the second dialogue, to describe a human being as the neediest of all animals, he says, *"Aspice nudum et informem inter vagitus et lacrimas nascentem."* He is clearly talking in the broadest terms about the human condition. Whereas Draper renders this "Behold him naked and unformed, born in wailings and tears," I say, "Just look at this human—naked and unformed, born crying and wailing" (page 82). Although "this human" is not expressed in the Latin, it seems to me more accurate than Draper's (perhaps more linguistically justifiable) "him."

Although my approach admittedly distances the translation from the structure of the original, I hope that the liberties I have taken will allow readers who are not necessarily familiar with the classical literary canon or with fourteenth-century Latin literature to experience both the complexities and the power of Petrarch's writing. My greatest hope is that students who are exposed to this power and these complexities will not stop with this version but will rather seek out and explore the original Latin text.

PART TWO

The Secret

PROLOGUE

I have often wondered how I came into the world and how I would leave it. While I was thinking about this recently (not in a dream as a feverish or sleeping person might, but wide-awake and with a clear head), I was shocked to see a woman, radiant with an indescribable light surrounding her. She possessed a beauty rarely seen among humankind. I could not tell her age or how she came to be there. From her clothes and appearance I judged her a virgin. Her eyes were like the sun, shining with rays of such powerful light that I lowered my own eyes before her, and I was afraid to look up.

When she saw this, she said, "Don't be afraid. Do not let my sudden and strange appearance alarm you in any way. I saw your steps had gone astray, and I felt compassion for you and have come down from afar to bring you help, which you clearly need. Until now you have turned your dull eyes far too much on the things of the earth. If these eyes, still so weak, have so delighted in mere mortal things, what will be your joy when you gaze on things eternal?"

I heard her say these words. Then, although I was still shaking with fear, I replied, my voice trembling, in Virgil's words: "By what name should I call you, maiden? For your face is hardly mortal, and your voice is not that of a human being."[1]

---

[1] Virgil, *Aeneid* I, 327–28.

"I am she," she said, "whom you have depicted with deliberate elegance in your poem *Africa,* and for whom you, with the energy of Amphion of Thebes, have built with stunning art and (so to speak) poetic hands a brilliant, beautiful palace in the far west on Atlas's highest peak. Don't be afraid, then, to listen and to look at me. For, as your finely wrought allegory proves, I have long been well known to you."[2]

Scarcely had she uttered these words when, as I considered all she had said, I realized that this could be none other than Truth herself. I remembered how I had described her palace on the heights of Atlas. I did not know from what region she had come, but I felt she must have come from heaven. Eager to see her, I looked up, but my human vision could not bear her ethereal light. Again, I lowered my eyes to the earth. She took note of this. After a short silence, she again spoke, and asking me many questions, she led me into a long conversation with her. From this conversation, I know I gained doubly: I won a little knowledge, and also the very act of talking with her gave me some measure of confidence. I found myself slowly becoming able to look at the face whose splendor had at first so scared me. Soon I was able to bear her radiance without dread, and I stared fixedly at her with great delight.

I then looked around to see if she was accompanied by anyone or if she had come to me alone. As I did, I saw at her side the figure of an aged man, venerable and majestic. There was no need to ask his name. His religious bearing, modest brow, his eyes full of dignity, his measured step, his African dress combined with Roman eloquence, all these plainly declared him to be that most illustrious father Augustine. So gracious and noble was his expression that one could not possibly imagine it belonged to any other. Even so I was about to speak up and ask who he was, when at that moment I heard his name, a sound so sweet to me, uttered from the lips of Truth herself. Turning toward him, and interrupting his deep meditation, she said, "Augustine, dear to me above a thousand others, you know how devoted this man here is to you. You know that he is stricken with a dangerous and persistent sickness, and that the farther he retreats from understanding his

---

[2] *Africa:* Petrarch's epic poem about Scipio Africanus, the Roman military and political leader who conquered Hannibal during the Second Punic War between Rome and Carthage. Interestingly, the poem as we have it does not contain the description of Truth's palace alluded to here. **Amphion of Thebes:** According to Greek mythology, Amphion was such a talented musician that his playing once made stones move by themselves to build a wall to fortify the city of Thebes. **Atlas:** The mountain on which, according to legend, the stars rest.

disease, the nearer he gets to death. This half-dead man needs care at once, and no one is better suited for this pious work than you. Your name has always been most dear to him, and lessons more easily enter the mind of a student who already loves the teacher. Furthermore, unless your present happiness has made you forget your former sorrow, you remember that when you were shut in the prison of the body, you suffered similar things. And so, as you are a most worthy physician for diseases from which you yourself suffered, I ask you, even though I know that of all things silent meditation is for you the most agreeable, please break your silence and try somehow to bring calm to this man who is so deeply distressed."

Augustine answered her, "You are my guide, my counselor, my ruler, my master: What, therefore would you have me say in your presence?"

She replied, "Let a human voice speak to a mortal ear. Then he will better bear the truth. But I will remain so that whatever you say to him he will take as said by me."

Augustine replied, "Both the love I feel for this sick man and the authority of the one bidding me urge me to obey." Then, looking kindly at me and embracing me as a father would, he led me away to a more private place, while Truth went on a few steps in front. There we all three sat down. While Truth, as the silent judge, listened and with no one else present, we talked back and forth, on and on, for three days. We discussed many things—the deplorable manners of the current age and the failings common to humankind—in such a way that the reproaches of the master seemed directed against people in general rather than at me alone. Yet those that seemed most applicable to me I impressed with special care on my memory.

That this conversation, so intimate and deep, should not be lost, I have written it down and made this book. I would not, however, classify it with my other works, nor do I desire any credit from it. My thoughts aim higher. What I desire is that through reading it, I may be able to renew as often as I wish the pleasure I took in the conversation itself. So, little book, I bid you to flee from public places. Be content to stay with me, true to the title that I have given you. For you are my secret, and thus you are titled. And when I think about profound subjects, speak to me in secret what has been in secret spoken to you.

To avoid the too frequent repetition of the words "I said" and "he said," and to make the drama of the dialogue vivid, I have used Cicero's method and merely placed the name of each interlocutor before each paragraph. Cicero in turn learned this technique from

Figure 4.   The Interlocutors in *The Secret.*

This manuscript, which contains various ethical writings including *The Secret,* was written in 1470 in Flanders for Jan Krabbe, the abbot of Ter Duinen, a monastery in Flanders. The illustration above the text shows Truth seated at the center with Franciscus standing to the right and Augustinus to the left. Behind Franciscus is the abbot for whom the manuscript was produced, with his entourage.

Brugge, Episcopal Seminary, ms. 113/78. Reprinted with permission.

Plato. But to cut short all further digression, this is how Augustine began the conversation.

FIRST DIALOGUE

Augustinus: What do you have to say for yourself, frail human? What are your dreams? Your hopes? Have you completely forgotten your miserable condition? Don't you remember that you are mortal?

Franciscus: Of course I remember it. Indeed, I shudder every time that thought comes into my mind.

Augustinus: If only you had remembered, as you claim, and taken heed! You would have spared me much trouble. For to recollect one's misery and to reflect frequently on death, these are the surest aids in scorning the seductions of this world and in ordering the soul amidst the tumult of earthly existence—provided, of course, that such reflection is not superficial, but rather sinks deep into the bones and marrow. But I am afraid that in this important matter you, like so many others, are deceiving yourself.

Franciscus: How, I ask you? I don't clearly understand what you are saying.

Augustinus: O race of mortals, this above all astonishes me and makes me afraid for you! You cling, of your own will, to your miseries, pretending that you do not know the peril hanging over your heads! And if this is brought to your attention, you thrust the warning aside.

Franciscus: How do we do this?

Augustinus: Do you think that there is anyone so deranged that if stricken with a critical illness, he would not wholeheartedly desire health?

Franciscus: No one is that demented.

Augustinus: And do you think that if one wished for a thing wholeheartedly, with all his soul, he would be so idle and careless not to use all possible means to obtain what he desired?

Franciscus: Surely not.

Augustinus: If we are agreed on these two points, we must also agree on a third.

Franciscus: What is this third point?

Augustinus: It is this: Just as someone who through deep meditation has discovered that he is miserable will desire to be so no more, and as someone who has formed this wish will seek to achieve it, so he who seeks will be able to reach what he wishes. But the third point depends on the second, as the second depends on the first. And therefore the first should be considered, as it were, the root of human salvation. But you humans don't think. Even you yourself, clever as you are, strive to your own detriment to pull this saving root out of your heart using the pleasures of the world. This fills me with horror and amazement. It is just, therefore, that you are punished through the loss of this root of salvation and consequently through the loss of everything else.

Franciscus: I can see that this complaint of yours is likely to be lengthy and to require many words. Would you mind, therefore, if we postpone it? May we now spend more time on your premises so that I might follow more securely to your conclusion?

Augustinus: I must accommodate your slowness, so please stop me at any point you wish.

Franciscus: Speaking for myself, I just don't see your argument.

Augustinus: What possible obscurity is there in it? What are you in doubt about now?

Franciscus: I believe that there is a multitude of things for which we ardently long, which we seek with all our energy, but which nevertheless, no matter how diligent we are, we have never obtained and never will.

Augustinus: That may be true of other desires, but in regard to what we are talking about now, the case is wholly different.

Franciscus: What makes you say that?

Augustinus: Because all those who desire to be delivered from their misery, provided only that they desire sincerely and with their whole hearts, cannot fail to get what they want.

Franciscus: Oh, no! What am I hearing? Few indeed are those who do not feel they lack many things. All who question their own hearts will acknowledge this and thus confess that they are unhappy. For if the most abundant accumulation of good things makes a person happy, then surely all the things that he lacks must make a person unhappy. And it is obvious that all would want to lay down this burden of unhappiness, but that few have been able to do this. How many are there who have felt the crushing weight of grief, through bodily disease, or the death of those they loved, or imprisonment, or exile, or poverty, or other misfortunes, it would take too long to recount; and yet they who suffer these things cannot simply cast them off. To me, then, it seems quite beyond dispute that many are unhappy unwillingly and in spite of themselves.

Augustinus: I must take you a long way back, and, as one does with young children whose attention wanders and whose wits are slow, I must reweave my argument for you from its simplest elements. I thought your mind was more advanced. I had no idea that you still needed lessons so childish. Ah, if only you had kept in mind those true and healthful maxims of the philosophers, which you have often read and reread with me; if, with all due respect, you had worked for yourself instead of for others; if you had but applied your study of so many tomes to the ruling of your own conduct instead of to vanity and to gaining the empty praise of others, you would not say such crude and absurd things.

Franciscus: I don't see exactly what you mean, but already I am aware of a blush rising to my cheeks, and I feel like schoolboys do in the presence of an angry master. Before they know what they are accused of, they think of many offenses of which they are guilty, and at the very first word from the master's lips, they are filled with confusion. Similarly, I too am conscious of my ignorance and of many other faults, and although I don't really follow the drift of your admonition, since I know that there is no charge that cannot be made against me, I blush even before you have finished speaking. So please, be explicit: What is this biting accusation that you have made?

Augustinus: I'll have more to say about that later. Just now what makes me so indignant is to hear you suppose that anyone can become or can be unhappy unwillingly.

Franciscus: I see I had no reason to blush. For what more obvious truth can possibly be imagined? Who is there who lives so ignorant or so far removed from all contact with the world as not to know that penury, grief, disgrace, illness, death, and other evils that are reckoned among the greatest often befall us in spite of ourselves, and never with our own consent? From which it follows that it is easy enough to recognize and to detest one's own misery, but not to end it; so that if the two first steps depend on ourselves, the third is nevertheless in the power of fortune.

Augustinus: Your shame was earning you forgiveness for your error, but now your impudence angers me more than your original mistake. How is it that you have forgotten all those wise precepts of philosophy, which declare that no one can be made unhappy by the things you were rattling off? For if virtue alone makes the soul happy, as has been demonstrated often through weighty arguments by Cicero and many others, it follows that nothing is opposed to happiness except what is also opposed to virtue. This truth you can yourself call to mind even without a word from me—unless, that is, your wits are very dull.

Franciscus: I remember it very well. You would have me bear in mind the precepts of the Stoics, which contradict the opinion of the crowd and are nearer to truth than to common custom.[3]

Augustinus: And you would indeed be the most miserable of all creatures were you to try to arrive at the truth through the rants of the crowd, or to suppose that with blind guides you would somehow reach the light. You must avoid the common beaten track and, aspiring higher, take the path marked by the steps of a very few if you are to merit hearing the poet's praise: "On, my son, with strength and virtue; thus is the path to the stars."[4]

Franciscus: Would that I earn that praise before I die! But please, go on. For I assure you I have by no means become shameless. I do not doubt that the Stoics' rules are far wiser than the errors of the crowd. I wait, therefore, for your further advice.

Augustinus: Since we are agreed that no one can become or be unhappy except through his own fault, what more needs to be said?

Franciscus: Just this: I think I have seen very many people, and I am one of them, for whom nothing is more distressing than the inability to break free of their faults, though all their lives they make the greatest efforts to do so. So, even if we grant that the maxim of the Stoics holds true, one may yet admit that many people are very unhappy in spite of themselves, unhappy even though they lament it and wish that they were not.

Augustinus: We wandered somewhat from our course, but we are slowly working our way back to our starting point. Or have you forgotten from where we set out?

Franciscus: I had begun to lose sight of it, but it's coming back to me now.

Augustinus: What I had set out to accomplish was to show you that the first step in avoiding the distress of this life and raising the soul to higher things is to meditate on death and the misery of the human condition, and that the second step is to have a passionate desire and eagerness to rise. When these two things are present, I

[3]**Stoics:** Followers of the philosophy of Zeno, which emphasized, among other things, duty, self-control, and the mastery of desire by the will as important elements of virtue and thus of happiness.

[4]Virgil, *Aeneid* IX, 641.

promised that the ascent toward our goal would be relatively easy. Unless it seems to you otherwise?

Franciscus: I wouldn't dare to imagine that it could be otherwise. Ever since I was a young man, I have had the growing conviction that if in any matter I was inclined to think differently from you, then I was certain to be wrong.

Augustinus: Please, I beg you, skip the flattery. I see that you are inclined to accept the truth of my words more out of deference than conviction. Instead, please feel free to express your true judgment.

Franciscus: I am still nervous about disagreeing with you, but I will make use of the liberty you grant. Leaving aside all others, my witnesses will be Truth, who has seen my every action, and also you. Many times I have reflected on my miserable condition and on my death. How I have sought to wash away my stains with a flood of tears! I can hardly speak of it without weeping. Yet to this point all has been in vain. This alone leads me to doubt the truth of the proposition you seek to establish, the proposition that no one has ever fallen into misery except by his own free will, or remained miserable except of his own accord. My own sad experience proves the opposite.

Augustinus: That complaint is an old one and likely to be unending. Though I have already stated the truth several times in vain, I shall not give up yet. No one can become unhappy or be unhappy unless he so chooses, but, as I said at the beginning, there is in humans a certain perverse and dangerous inclination to deceive themselves, which is the most deadly thing in life. For if we justly fear the machinations of those close to us, both because the respect we have for them erases our suspicions and because their sweet, familiar voices resound in our ears (things that do not come into play with strangers), how much more ought you to fear the deceptions you practice on yourself! Here love, respect, and familiarity play a huge part, since people think more of themselves than they deserve and love themselves more than they ought. And here deceiver and deceived are the same person.

Franciscus: You have said this kind of thing often today already. But I do not recall ever practicing such deception on myself, and I hope other people have not deceived me either.

Augustinus: Now at this very moment, when you are greatly deceiving yourself, you boast that you have never deceived yourself. And I have enough trust in your wit and talent to believe that if you pay close attention, you will see that no one can ever fall into misery except through his own free will. For on this point our whole debate rests. Tell me, therefore—but please think before you answer, and let your soul long for truth, not disputation—tell me: What person do you think was forced to sin? The wise require that sin be a voluntary action, and so rigid is their definition that if this voluntariness is not there, then sin is not there either. But without sin, no one is made unhappy, as you agreed to admit a few minutes ago.

Franciscus: I see that slowly I am getting away from my proposition and am being compelled to acknowledge that the beginning of my misery did arise from my own will. I feel it is true in myself, and I imagine it is true for others. Now I ask that you, for your part, also acknowledge a certain truth.

Augustinus: What is it that you want me to acknowledge?

Franciscus: That as it is true that no one ever fell into misery except voluntarily, so it is also true that countless of those who have thus voluntarily fallen nevertheless do not voluntarily remain miserable. This is most certainly true in my own case. In fact, I think that I have received this as punishment: Because I would not stand firm when I was able, so now I cannot rise when I wish to.

Augustinus: Although that opinion is not completely unreasonable, nonetheless inasmuch as you realize that you were wrong in your first proposition, so I think you must admit that you are wrong in your second.

Franciscus: So you would say that there is no distinction between "to fall" and "to remain"?

Augustinus: No, they are different. But after all, with respect to time, "to have desired" and "to desire" are also different; nonetheless, in essential meaning and in the mind of the one who desires, they are one and the same.

Franciscus: I see in what knots you entangle me. But the wrestler who wins victory by a trick is not necessarily stronger, though he may be more crafty.

Augustinus: We speak before Truth herself. To her, complete simplicity is a dear friend, and cunning is an enemy. And in order for you to see this clearly, let us go forward from this point with as much clarification as you desire.

Franciscus: You could give me no news more welcome. Tell me, then, since we are talking about my own self, through what line of reasoning you are going to prove that I am unhappy and that I remain so by my own consent. That I am unhappy I do not deny. But that I remain so by consent? On the contrary, I feel that nothing could be more hateful and more opposed to my own will. Yet I am not able to do anything more.

Augustinus: If the agreements we have already made are preserved, I will show you that you should use different words.

Franciscus: What agreements do you mean, and what words would you have me use?

Augustinus: The agreements are that, having rejected the snares of deception, we devote ourselves, with pure simplicity, to the pursuit of truth. And as for the words that I would have you use, they are these: Where you said that you *cannot* do anything more, you should say that you *will not* do anything more.

Franciscus: There will be no end, then, to our discussion, for that is what I shall never confess. I tell you I know, and you yourself are a witness to this, how often I have "wanted" but "was not able" to act, how many tears I have shed, and they have profited me nothing.

Augustinus: Oh, yes, I have seen many tears, but no will at all.

Franciscus: Alas, heaven knows! But I think that no mortal knows what I have suffered and how I have longed to rise up, if it were only possible, to higher things.

Augustinus: Quiet! Heaven and earth will crash in ruin, the stars themselves will fall to the underworld, and all harmonious nature be divided against itself before Truth, who is our judge, can be deceived.

Franciscus: And what do you mean by that?

Augustinus: I mean that your tears have often racked your conscience but not changed your will.

Franciscus: How many times have I said that I can do nothing further?

Augustinus: And how many times have I responded that rather you *want* to do nothing further? Still, I am not surprised that you find yourself entangled in these complexities, by which once I myself was tormented, when I was thinking about taking up a new way of life. I tore my hair, I beat my forehead, and I wrung my hands. At last, wrapping my arms around my knees, I filled the air and the heavens with most bitter sighs, and I drenched the earth with copious tears. Yet through all these things, I remained the same man I was, until deep meditation at last heaped up before my eyes all my misery. And then after I desired completely to change, I was also instantly able, and with miraculous and most welcome speed I was transformed into another Augustine, whose life story, unless I am mistaken, you know from my *Confessions*.[5]

Franciscus: Certainly, I know it, and I cannot forget that health-bringing fig tree under whose shade the miracle took place.

Augustinus: It is right that you remember it. And further, no tree should be more dear to you; no myrtle, no ivy, nor even the laurel loved, they say, by Apollo.[6] True, this laurel tree above others is favored by the whole chorus of poets and by you too, you who alone in your age have deserved to wear a crown woven of its leaves. Yet dearer to you than this and all these others should be the memory of that fig tree, finally returning you into port after so many storms, a memory through which sure hope of correction and forgiveness is foretold to you.

Franciscus: I object to none of this. Please, go on with what you have begun.

Augustinus: This is what I began and what I now argue: Up until now, what has happened to you has happened to many, of whom it can be said in that verse of Virgil's, "The mind remains unmoved, fruitless tears pour down."[7] Although I could have gathered many illustrations about this, nonetheless I was content with this single example that is particularly familiar to you.

Franciscus: You have chosen wisely. For your case did not need more, nor could another example have penetrated more deeply into my heart. This is all the more true because, although we are separated by the greatest distance, as great as that between a shipwrecked person and one who possesses a safe port, or between a happy person and a miserable one, still somehow within my inner turmoil I recognize a vestige of your wrenching struggle. As a result, it happens that whenever I read your book the *Confessions*—caught between two contrary feelings, namely hope and fear, sometimes with tears of joy—I think that I am reading the story not of

[5]Augustinus is alluding to the description in the *Confessions* of his anguish immediately before his conversion experience, which took place in a garden under a fig tree. In the *Confessions,* however, Augustine describes the change in his will not as the result of the intensity of his desire, but rather as an effect of God's grace, which acts on him as he reads a passage from Saint Paul's letters.

[6]**Apollo:** Son of Zeus and Leto, Apollo was among the most revered Greek gods. The laurel tree was his favorite because when he pursued Daphne, whose beauty had captivated him, she prayed for aid and was transformed into a laurel tree to prevent him from capturing her. For unrelated reasons, the laurel is also associated with poetry. Petrarch was crowned as poet laureate with a laurel wreath in Rome in 1341.

[7]Virgil, *Aeneid* IV, 449.

another's wanderings but of my very own. At this point, then, as I have cast aside all desire for dispute, please proceed as you like. I am ready to follow rather than hinder you.

Augustinus: I make no such demand of you. For, just as a certain most learned man said, "Through excessive quarreling the truth is lost,"[8] so moderate debate leads many to the truth. It is not then expedient to accept everything advanced, which is the hallmark of a slack and lazy mind, any more than it is expedient to contend vehemently with an obvious truth, which is a clear sign of an overly litigious mind.

Franciscus: I understand and agree and will act on your advice. Please, go on.

Augustinus: You then recognize, of course, that the argument is true and the chain of reasoning valid, that a perfect understanding of one's misery produces a perfect desire to rise up above it? The power to do this follows the desire.

Franciscus: I have resolved already in my soul that I will believe everything you say.

Augustinus: I sense that something is still bothering you. Let's hear it, whatever it is.

Franciscus: Nothing, except that I am shocked [to hear] that up until now, I have never wanted what I believed I had always wanted.

Augustinus: You still don't follow! But in order that this conversation might someday finally end, I concede that sometimes you have wanted what you believe you have always wanted.

Franciscus: So what is your argument?

Augustinus: Doesn't the saying of Ovid come to mind: "To want [Latin verb *velle*] is not enough; if you are to possess something, it is necessary that you long for it [Latin verb *cupere*]."[9]

Franciscus: I understand that, but I thought I was yearning *[desiderare]* for it.

Augustinus: You were wrong.

Franciscus: So I see.

Augustinus: To see this more clearly, examine your conscience. That

---

[8]Publilius, quoted in Aulus Gellius, *Attic Nights* XVII, 14. Gellius (ca. 123–169 C.E.) studied in Rome and Athens. He began to compile the *Attic Nights,* a collection of linguistic and historical notes, anecdotes, and stories taken from a range of ancient authors, while living in Athens. *Attica* was the term used to describe the area of Greece around Athens, hence the title *Attic Nights.*

[9]Ovid, *Letters from the Black Sea* III, 1, 35. These letters were written while Ovid was living in exile in the town of Tomis.

faculty is the best interpreter of virtue. It is the infallible and true evaluator of thoughts and actions. Your conscience will tell you that you have never longed to attain salvation as you should, but only more halfheartedly and more lazily than your extremely perilous situation warranted.

Franciscus: I have begun to inspect my conscience, as you suggest.

Augustinus: What do you find there?

Franciscus: The things you say are true.

Augustinus: We have made a little progress. I see you are beginning to wake up. Now the situation will be better for you if you recognize how bad it once was.

Franciscus: If it is enough only to acknowledge this, then I am confident that soon my situation can be not only good but great. For I have understood nothing more clearly than that I have never desired *[optare]* liberty and an end to misery ardently enough. But perhaps from now on it will be enough to desire *[optare]?*

Augustinus: Enough for what?

Franciscus: I mean, it will be enough to desire without doing anything else.

Augustinus: What you propose is impossible, namely that one who ardently desires *[cupere]* what he is able to pursue goes to sleep.

Franciscus: What, then, is the specific benefit of desire?

Augustinus: Certainly, it opens a path in the midst of obstacles. And furthermore, the desire for virtue is itself a great part of virtue.

Franciscus: You have offered me cause for real hope.

Augustinus: I speak with you in order to teach you to hope and to fear.

Franciscus: To fear in what way?

Augustinus: Rather, you tell me, how to hope?

Franciscus: You want to teach me this because, although up until now I have acted, with no small effort, so as not to become the worst, you open a way through which I might become the best.

Augustinus: But maybe you do not understand how arduous that way is.

Franciscus: Why do you repeat these new terrors? Why do you say the path is so arduous?

Augustinus: Because this term "to desire" *[optare]* is one word, but it consists of innumerable things.

Franciscus: You are scaring me.

Augustinus: And even if we leave aside the elements out of which desire is composed, how many are the things by whose destruction desire is produced!

Franciscus: I don't understand what you are trying *[velle]* to say.

Augustinus: This kind of desire *[desiderium]* that I am describing can exist for no thing unless it has put an end to all other desires. For you understand how many and diverse the things are that we long for *[optare]* in life. All these things must first be esteemed as nothing if you would rise up toward a yearning *[concupiscentia]* for the highest happiness. The person surely loves *[amare]* this happiness less who loves something else *along with* it that he does not love *on account of* it.

Franciscus: I recognize the argument.

Augustinus: How many people are there, really, who have extinguished all desires—which are hard even to list, let alone extinguish—who have brought the bridle of reason to their souls, who would dare to say, "Now I have nothing in common with the body; all visible things have grown dirty; I long for happier things"?

Franciscus: That kind of person is most rare, and now I understand the difficulty with which you threatened me.

Augustinus: And even if these desires *[cupiditas]* all cease, that other desire *[desiderium]* will not be full and at hand. For as the soul is carried toward heaven by its own nobility, so it is with equal force pulled down by the weight of the body and by earthly allurements *[illecebra]*. And so, as you desire both to rise and to stay in the lowest places, you fulfill neither, always distracted from one by the other.

Franciscus: What, then, do you think must be done so that the whole soul, breaking its chains to the earth, might rise to the greatest heights?

Augustinus: What leads to this goal is, surely, that meditation [on death] that I described in the first place, along with the continual recollection of your mortality.

Franciscus: Unless I am wrong about this too, no person is more often preoccupied with these concerns than I.

Augustinus: A new quarrel, another task.

Franciscus: What? Am I also lying about this?

Augustinus: I would like to speak more elegantly.

Franciscus: But say the same thing.

Augustinus: Exactly.

Franciscus: So you are saying that I don't think about death?

Augustinus: Only very rarely, and so sluggishly that your thinking never gets to the core of the problem.

Franciscus: I thought just the opposite.

Augustinus: I care not about what you have thought, but about what you should have thought.

Franciscus: Know that from now on I will never trust myself if you prove that I have been wrong about this.

Augustinus: I will prove it with great ease if only you resolve in good faith to acknowledge the truth in your soul. To do this, I will use a witness who is close at hand.

Franciscus: Who, may I ask?

Augustinus: Your conscience.

Franciscus: It says the opposite.

Augustinus: When the question posed is confused, the testimony of the respondent can hardly be certain.

Franciscus: What does that have to do with anything?

Augustinus: A lot, obviously. Listen so that you can understand clearly. No one is so demented, unless he is truly insane, that he is oblivious to his own fragile condition. There is no one who would not respond, if asked, that he was mortal and that he inhabited a fallen body. Furthermore, our bodily pains and the trials of disease attest to this. Will the indulgence of any God ever allow a life to be lived immune to these? And what of the funerals of our friends, which pass incessantly before our eyes, so that terror arises in the souls of those watching? When one buries a contemporary, one cannot but tremble at the suddenness of that one's death and begin to worry about oneself. Just as after you have seen your neighbors' roofs burning, you cannot rest easy about your own, because, as Horace says, "you understand that before long dangers will come to you."[10]

He will be all the more moved who sees a person younger, stronger, and more beautiful than himself taken away by sudden death. For in this case he will look around and say to himself, "That person seemed to live securely, and nonetheless he has been snatched away, and neither youth, nor beauty, nor health was of any use to him. Who has promised me security? A god? Some magician? In the end, I am surely mortal." And if this same fate befalls emperors and kings of the earth, if it befalls exceptional and formidable people, then those close by are even more vehemently shaken when they unexpectedly see, perhaps within a few hours, someone with a reputation for cowing others himself prostrate with cares. Aren't these very feelings the source of the actions that the stunned populace takes upon the death of the most powerful

---

[10] Horace, *Letters* I, 18, 83. The quotation is not exact.

among them, the sort of actions that you (if I might recall you for a time to the deeds of history) remember happened at the funeral of Julius Caesar?[11] It is this communal spectacle that seizes the eyes and hearts of mortals. As they see another's fate they are reminded of their own. Fury befalls us, the fury of beasts and humans, the rages of war; great buildings fall to ruins, and structures that, as someone rightly says, had been the protector of men now become a threat. To these are added dangerous winds from an evil star, the gusts of a pestilential sky, and so many perils on land and sea. Because of all these, no matter where you turn your eyes, you cannot but see an image of your own mortality.

Franciscus: Enough, please. I can't take any more of this. I think that nothing more efficacious could be said to strengthen my reason than the many things you have already said. And as I was listening to you, I wondered what the aim of your words could be and where this speech was headed.

Augustinus: Well, it certainly wasn't yet finished when you cut it short. It lacked this conclusion: Although many reminders and provocations surround you humans (nonetheless nothing penetrates to the inner core, as your suffering hearts have through long habit been hardened and, like an old callus, are resistant to salutary admonitions), you will find few who sufficiently ponder their own inevitable death.

Franciscus: So there are few who have really grasped the definition of a human, which is repeated so frequently in all schools that it must not only have wearied the ears of the listeners but even worn out the columns of the buildings?

Augustinus: Certainly, this kind of babbling among dialecticians[12] will never come to an end. It throws up summaries of definitions like this one of "man," and it boasts material for eternal controversies. However, when it comes to the real truth of the things of which they speak, these dialecticians for the most part know nothing. If you ask one from this crowd about the definition of a man or of anything else, his answer is ready. If you ask him to elaborate, there will be only silence, or if his long familiarity with arguing brings forth audacity and many words, his very way of speaking will demonstrate that he has no true knowledge of the thing he just

---

[11] Suetonius, *Lives of the Caesars* 84–85.

[12] **dialecticians:** University-trained scholastic philosophers who used a highly specialized, technical vocabulary and method to investigate questions that Petrarch often considered overly pedantic or irrelevant.

defined. Against this breed of men, with their cultivated ignorance and useless curiosity, it is good to protest, "Why do you labor endlessly for nothing, you miserable creatures; why exercise your mind on inane subtleties? Why, forgetful of actual things, do you grow old among words? Why do you remain, as your hair turns white and your brows wrinkle, preoccupied with these childish games? Would that your madness hurt only yourselves and had not so often corrupted the finest minds among the young!"

Franciscus: I believe that nothing can be said too harshly against these perverse studies. But you, meanwhile, carried away by your zeal, have left unfinished what you started to say about the definition of man.

Augustinus: I thought enough had been said, but I will be more explicit. Man is an animal, indeed the first among all animals. Even the densest rustic knows that much. Further, no one, if asked, would deny that man is both rational and mortal.

Franciscus: Yes, this definition is known to everyone.

Augustinus: No. Rather, it is known by only a very, very few.

Franciscus: How is that so?

Augustinus: If you see someone who is directed by reason to such a degree that he lives his life according to it, that he subjects his appetites to it alone, that reason's bridle restrains the movements of his soul; if you see someone so directed by reason that he understands that through this only does he distinguish himself from the savagery of brute animals, who understands that he deserves to be called by the name of human only to the extent that he lives according to reason; if you see a man sufficiently aware of his own mortality that he keeps this before his eyes every day and restrains himself because of it; a man who, despising the transitory things of the world, longs for that life where, greatly endowed with reason, he will cease to be mortal; if you see such a one as this, then, at last, you can say that he has a true and useful grasp of the definition of a human being. This last subject is the topic of our conversation. I said that few people have obtained sufficient understanding of it or familiarity with it.

Franciscus: Until now I thought that I was such a man.

Augustinus: And I do not doubt that, as you think about both the many things you have learned from experience in life and the things you have learned from reading books, thoughts of death frequently occur to you. But these have never penetrated deeply enough, nor have they taken hold tenaciously.

Franciscus: What do you mean by "penetrated deeply"? Although I think I understand, I still wish to hear more clearly from you what you mean.

Augustinus: I will tell you (although by now everyone has accepted this, and furthermore the best witnesses from among the philosophers agree as well). I mean that of all things that inspire fear, death is the first and most dreadful, so much so that the very word *death* has for a long time seemed loathsome and harsh to our ears. Nonetheless, we should not allow either the syllables of the word or the memory of the thing itself to pass quickly from our minds. Rather, we must spend time thinking about it; we must with keen attention picture one by one the body parts of the dying: While the extremities grow cold, the breast burns and sweats with fever, the abdomen throbs with pain, the vital spirit gets slower and slower with the coming of death; the eyes sunken and swimming, the tearful gaze, the forehead pale and drawn, the hollow cheeks, the blackened teeth, the nostrils shrunken and sharpened, lips foaming, the tongue slow and scaly, the mouth dry, the languid head and gasping breast, the hoarse voice and mournful sigh, the evil smell of the whole body, above all the horror of a face one cannot recognize.

All of these things will come more easily to mind and be ready to hand if we have closely observed a memorable example of a real death; for a memory of something seen is usually more tenacious than one of something heard. For this reason, and not without sound rationale, in certain devout and most holy religious orders, even down to our own time, which despises sound habits, that custom endures according to which those who profess the strict way of life are present to see the bodies of the dead while they are washed and prepared for burial, so that the sad and deplorable spectacle, thrust before their eyes, might always admonish them to remember and also drive the surviving souls away from retaining any hope in this fleeting world.

This, then, is what I call "penetrated deeply enough," not when you say the word *death* out of habit or when you repeat, "Nothing is more certain than the fact of death, nothing less certain than its hour," and other truisms of this kind that we hear every day. Such words just fly away; they don't sink down deeply and stay with you.

Franciscus: I accept your advice more easily because, as you speak, I recognize many things that I often think about in silence. Nonetheless, please put some marker in my memory that will remind me from now on not to lie to myself or to delude myself about my failings. For I think this is what turns the minds of men away from the path of virtue: When they think they have reached their goal, they strive no further.

Augustinus: I am glad to hear you say that, for these are the words not of a lazy and fatalistic person, but of a thoughtful soul. Therefore, here is a test that will never deceive you. If when you think about death, you remain still and quiet, know that you are meditating in vain, as if you were thinking about other less important things. But if in the act of meditation, you suddenly stiffen, tremble, and grow pale; if you seem already to suffer amidst the pains of death; if your soul seems to leave your body and you feel yourself at the bar of eternal judgment, where you must render an exact account of all the words and actions of your whole past life; if you sense that nothing more is to be hoped for from wit or eloquence, nothing from wealth or power, nothing from physical beauty or worldly glory; this judge cannot be bought, nor deceived, nor placated. If you feel that death marks not an end to suffering but a passage, one that goes through a thousand kinds of punishments: the noise and groans of Avernus, and the sulfurous rivers, and the darkness, and the avenging Furies—in short, the unrelenting barbarity of deadly Orcus;[13] and what is the climax of all these horrors, that this perpetual unhappiness and this hopelessness will never end, and the anger of God, no longer compassionate, will endure forever; if all these things rise simultaneously before your eyes, not as fiction but as truth, not as remote possibilities but as necessary and inevitable and imminent future events; and if you think about such things not lightly nor in desperation but full of hope that the hand of God is powerful and ready to lift you out of such evils if only you show yourself ready to be healed and eager to rise; if you remain committed and persistent in your resolve; *then* be assured that you have not meditated in vain.

Franciscus: I confess that you have truly terrified me by putting so huge a mass of suffering before my eyes. But may God's forgiveness be such that I immerse myself in these thoughts day after day and especially during the night, when the mind, eased of its daily

---

[13]**Avernus:** Lake Avernus in southern Italy; the name was understood to mean "without birds," and the lake was imagined to emit toxic fumes that would kill anything flying over it. In the *Aeneid,* Virgil uses Lake Avernus to mark the entrance to the underworld. **Furies:** Three goddesses of vengeance who, according to Greek and Roman mythology, lived in the underworld. **Orcus:** Hades, god of the underworld, who is also called Dis.

cares, can return to itself. At that time, when my body lies as the dying lie and my mind focuses on the hour of death and all its attendant horrors, I imagine this so intently that, feeling myself in the grips of death, I seem to discern Tartarus and all the evil things you speak of; and I am shaken by this vision so profoundly that, terrified and trembling, I rise up and, often to the terror of those near me, cry out these words: "What am I doing? What suffering is this? What kind of death does fate plan for me? Have mercy on me, Jesus, help me. 'Take me, unconquered one, from these evils. . . . ' 'Give your right hand to this miserable creature, and carry me with you through the waves, so that at least in death I may rest in a peaceful place.' "[14] I say these things and many others to myself just like a delirious person whose wandering and fearful mind is moved by every impulse. And I speak also to my friends, in whom my crying sometimes induces tears, although after the tears we all return to the way we were before. Since this is how it is, what keeps me back? What is the hidden obstacle because of which, up until now, my meditations have caused me nothing but troubles and terrors? And I am the same as I was before, the same even as are those who have never experienced in their lives anything like what I have described. And I am more miserable than those who, whatever kind of death their futures might bring, at least enjoy present pleasures. As for me, my end is uncertain, and no pleasure comes to me unless clouded by such bitterness.

Augustinus: Do not, please, grieve when there is reason to rejoice. For a sinner who takes great pleasure and delight in his crimes must be judged all the more miserable and vulnerable to harm.

Franciscus: I suppose this is so because a person whose own uninterrupted pleasure never ends in grief is never directed back to the path of virtue. But a person who, amid carnal delights and pleasures, undergoes some hardship of fortune, this person remembers his real condition insofar as that thoughtless and ill-advised state of delight deserts him. Still, if both ways of life end up in the same place, then I do not understand why the one who, although he will suffer later, rejoices now is not called happier than the one who neither feels happiness in the present nor expects to feel it. Unless perhaps you think that the one who now laughs will mourn more bitterly later?

Augustinus: Yes, much more bitterly, because when the rein of reason

[14] Virgil, *Aeneid* VI, 365, 370–71.

is completely thrown down, as happens with the highest kind of pleasure, the fall is more serious than a fall from the same height of one who keeps some hold, however feeble, on the rein. But above all, I attach importance to what you said before, that in the case of the one there is some hope of conversion, but in the case of the other there is only despair.

Franciscus: I think that too. But in the meantime, haven't you forgotten my initial question?

Augustinus: What?

Franciscus: I asked, "What holds me back?" Why am I the only one for whom intense meditation on death, which you say is so useful, serves no purpose?

Augustinus: This is because, in the first place, you think of death as something remote, whereas, given how short life is and the many kinds of accidents that can happen, it cannot be far off. In this, as Cicero says, "We almost all delude ourselves because we see death from far away."[15] Some correctors, or, more accurately, corrupters, of this passage have changed it by adding a negative before the verb, claiming that it should say "because we *don't* see death from far away." But who in their right mind is wholly unaware of the inevitability of death? Furthermore, Cicero's word *prospicere* does mean "to see from far away."

The one thing with regard to thinking about death that really has fooled many is this: While each has imagined for himself a life span that is conceivable, only a very few actually live this long. For perhaps no one ever dies to whom these verses do not apply: "He had expected gray hair and long years for himself."[16] This sentiment was able to hurt you, for your age and your healthy complexion and your modest way of life offered you this hope.

Franciscus: Please do not think such things about me. May God turn me from this madness, "lest I trust in this monster," as that most famous master of the sea says in Virgil's poem.[17] I, too, tossed about in a huge, cruel, violent sea, I steer a shaking, leaky, creaking boat through huge waves while the winds bear down against me. I know that this tiny craft cannot hold out for long, and I see no hope for safety remains, unless a merciful, all-powerful being makes it so

---

[15] Not Cicero but Seneca, *Moral Letters to Lucilius* 1, 2. The manuscript tradition of these letters supports the correction *"non prospicimus,"* which Augustinus disputes.

[16] Virgil, *Aeneid* X, 549.

[17] Ibid., V, 849. The master of the sea is Palinurus, pilot of Aeneas's ship in the *Aeneid*.

that I find the strength to turn the rudder and reach shore before I perish; then he who lived at sea will die in port. I owe it to this opinion that I have never ardently longed for the great wealth and power by which many people, not only my contemporaries but old men and those who have surpassed the common span of life, are consumed. For what folly would it be to spend one's whole life in toil and poverty, so that one might suddenly die worrying about conserving this wealth? And so I think about these dreadful events not as if they were far in the future, but as if they were to happen soon, indeed as if they were about to happen now. Nor have I forgotten a little verse that I wrote when I was young and that, among other things, I sent to a friend, adding this at the end: "Even while we are speaking about these things, perhaps death, rushed along countless paths, stands on our doorstep."[18] If I could speak those words then, in my youth, how will I speak now, when I am older and more experienced in life? Whatever I see and hear, whatever I feel or think, I understand it in the light of this one point, the imminence of death. So, unless I am wrong, the question "What holds me back?" still remains unaddressed.

Augustinus: Give humble thanks to God, who deigns to restrain you with such health-giving reins and who urges you on with sharp prodding. For it would hardly be possible that a person so frequently and vividly gripped by thoughts of death could be touched by eternal death. But because you feel, not without reason, that you lack something, I will try to show you what it is, so that, God willing, with that obstacle out of the way, your whole being can rise to these thoughts and can shake off the old yoke of servitude by which until now you have been held down.

Franciscus: If only you can do that, if only I am found capable of receiving such a gift!

Augustinus: If you want it, it shall be yours, for our task is not impossible. But with regard to human actions, two things are needed. If one or the other is lacking, the outcome will be thwarted. Thus the will must be ready to hand, and with such vehemence that it deserves to be called "desire."

Franciscus: It will be so.

Augustinus: Do you know what stands in the way of your meditations?

Franciscus: This is what I keep asking; this is what I so desperately want to know.

---

[18]It is not clear from Petrarch's extant works to what (if anything) this refers.

Augustinus: Then listen. Do not doubt that your soul, although it originated in heaven, has degenerated significantly from its original
nobility because of the contamination caused by contact with the
body in which it is enclosed. Indeed, the soul has not only degenerated, it has, after so much time, become numb. It has been made to
forget its own origin and supernatural maker. Certainly, Virgil,
inspired from above, seemed to refer to the passions that arise as
the soul melds with the body and forgets its better nature when he
said: "Fiery energy and a heavenly origin dwell within those generative seeds [of living creatures], to the degree that they are not
impeded by poisonous bodies or dulled by limbs of flesh. From this
they fear and desire, they grieve and rejoice. Enclosed in darkness
and a pitch-black prison, they do not see the heavens."[19] Do you see
in these verses that four-headed monster so opposed to humankind?

Franciscus: I very clearly see the fourfold passions of the soul, which
first are divided into two parts according to time, present or future,
and then are further distinguished according to the concepts of
good and evil. And so, because of these four as it were contrary
winds, the tranquillity of the human mind perishes.

Augustinus: You perceive this rightly, and the words of the apostle are
verified by our experience: "The body, which is corrupt, aggravates
the soul, and earthly existence presses in on the mind, which is taking in many things."[20] For innumerable shapes and images of visible
things, which entered through the bodily senses one at a time,
come together and crowd into the innermost parts of the soul. And
the soul, not made for this and not able to take in so many different
images, gets weighed down and confused. And so that plague of
apparitions rips and mangles your thinking, and with its fatal multi-
plicity obstructs the way to illuminating meditation, through which
we are raised up to the one and only highest light.

Franciscus: You wrote about that plague with great clarity in several
places and in particular in the book *On True Religion,* which scorns
it utterly. Recently, I came upon that book, having veered away
from reading poets and philosophers, and I read it intently and
eagerly. I was like a traveler, far from his homeland and eager to
see the world, who, crossing the unfamiliar border of some famous
city, is captivated by the sweetness of the sights and stops frequently here and there to study everything he sees.

[19]Virgil, *Aeneid* VI, 730–34.
[20]Although Franciscus attributes these words to the Apostle (that is, Paul), in fact
they are from Wisdom 9:15.

Augustinus: And yet, although it uses different words that are appropriate for someone like me, a teacher of Catholic truth, the teaching that you find in my book *On True Religion* is, for the most part, philosophical and especially Socratic and Platonic. And, lest I keep anything from you, you should know that I was led to begin this book primarily by a passage from your Cicero. God helped me with this undertaking, so that from a few seeds arose an abundant harvest. But let's return to the point of our conversation.

Franciscus: As you wish, beloved father, but one thing first. Please do not keep from me that specific passage in Cicero that provided the material for such an eloquent work.

Augustinus: In one of his works, Cicero, despising the errors of his time, says, "They could see nothing with the soul; they interpreted everything through the eyes. For only great intellects can recall the mind from the senses and direct their thinking away from the commonplace."[21] This is what Cicero said. I then took this as a foundation and built on it the work called *On True Religion,* which you say pleased you.

Franciscus: I know the passage. It's in Cicero's *Tusculan Disputations.* And I have noticed that here and there in your own works, you take delight in this passage of Cicero's—not without reason, for this is the kind of passage in which we find truth mixed with beauty and dignity. But let's get back to our discussion.

Augustinus: This, then, is the plague that has injured you, and unless you do something, it will quickly drive you to destruction. Overwhelmed by many different impressions and oppressed relentlessly by conflicting cares, your fragile soul cannot figure out what to do first, which thought to nourish, which to destroy, which to push away. Not even all of its strength and all of its time, what little of it we are granted, can handle so many demands. And just as many seeds planted in a small space impede each other's growth, so in your overcrowded soul nothing useful can take root, nothing can flourish to bear fruit. And, lacking any plan, you are pulled first to this, then that, but you never commit your full attention to anything. And so whenever your mind, which is by nature noble, has arrived at the thought of death and at other thoughts that might direct it toward life, and is through its natural acumen delving into the most profound things, it isn't strong enough to stand there, and

---

[21]Cicero, *Tusculan Disputations* I, 16, 37–38. Augustine never directly quotes this passage, and *On True Religion* contains very few direct references to Cicero.

as the turmoil of various problems assault it, the mind turns back. And so the healthy resolve shatters to pieces from excessive mobility, and there arises that internal discord about which we have already spoken at length, and the anxiety of a soul angry with itself, a soul that recoils from its filth yet does not purify itself, a soul that recognizes its own tortuous paths yet does not desert them, a soul that fears impending danger but does not turn away.

Franciscus: Ah, woe is me! Now you have probed deeply into my wound. There is where my misery dwells; because of this, I fear death.

Augustinus: Things are finally going well! You have shed your laziness. But because we have already talked enough for today without a break, we can, if you agree, put off the rest until tomorrow. Now let us rest for a while in silence.

Franciscus: I am tired. I would gratefully welcome rest and silence.

SECOND DIALOGUE

Augustinus: Well, have we rested long enough?

Franciscus: As you wish.

Augustinus: How are you doing? Are you feeling confident? Because hope in one who is sick is a significant sign of returning health.

Franciscus: What hope I have does not come from within myself. God is my hope.

Augustinus: You speak wisely. Now let's get back to the matter at hand. Many things besiege you, many things clamor around you, and as for you, you ignore both the number and the strength of the enemies that surround you. So I fear that you will suffer the usual fate of a person who discerns the ordered front line of an army from far away: Scornful of what appears to be their meager number, he makes an error in judgment. But as they get closer, and the soldiers, now right before his eyes, spread out, his fear grows and he regrets that he was initially less afraid than he should have been. It will be the same with you. When I force you to confront the many evils pressing in on you and walling you in from all sides, you will be ashamed that you were less afraid and less sad than you should have been, and you will hardly wonder that your soul, attacked by so many things, cannot break through the battle lines of its enemies. You will surely see how many opposing thoughts have smothered that single healthy one.

Franciscus: Now I am very frightened. I have always recognized that my danger is great. Now you say that this danger so far exceeds my estimation of it that, compared to how afraid I should be, I have hardly felt fear at all. What hope, then, could possibly remain for me?

Augustinus: Despair is the ultimate evil. Those who have succumbed to it have done so too hastily. Therefore, above all else, know this: Nothing merits despair.

Franciscus: I knew that, but my terror wiped out the memory.

Augustinus: Now turn your eyes and your soul toward me and, if I might use the words of a poet most familiar to you, "behold what populations gather round, what cities close their gates and sharpen the sword to kill you and your people."[22] See what snares the world holds out to you, how many vain hopes circle around you, how many empty cares press in on you. First, if I might start at the beginning, you must take care with all diligence lest you fall from the same sin that has, since the beginning of time, brought down the most noble of spirits. How many things there are that urge your soul to dangerous flights! How many that use the pretext of the soul's innate nobility to wear it down, making it forget how often it has experienced firsthand its own fragility! These things preoccupy the soul; they circle around it; they do not allow it to think of anything else. They make the soul proud and confident in its own powers; they make it so pleased with itself that it despises its creator. But, however grand these powers may be and whatever qualities you imagine yourself to possess, nonetheless these ought to induce in you not pride but humility, a humility that acknowledges that these remarkable qualities came to you through no merit of your own. For, leaving aside the case of an eternal ruler, what makes subjects more compliant to a temporal lord than spontaneous displays of generosity that were not triggered by any merit of their own? For they are eager to live up to the reward they ought to have worked to earn.

Now you can understand how insignificant are the things in which you take pride. You trust in your intellect and in your reading of many books. You boast of your eloquence, and you delight in the form of your body, which will soon be lifeless. Yet how many times your intellect fails you, how many are the arts in which your ability does not equal the most humble of humankind! I can go

[22]Virgil, *Aeneid* VIII, 385–86, except the *Aeneid* has "to kill me and my people."

further. There are meek and small animals whose work you could not imitate, not with any amount of effort. And still you boast about your intellect!

And what good has all your reading done you? Out of all the things you have read, how much has really stayed in your soul, what roots have grown there that will, in good time, bring forth fruit? Examine your heart carefully. If you compare the whole of what you know with what you don't know, you will find that your knowledge is like a small stream dried up in the summer heat compared to the ocean of your ignorance. And even granted that you do know a lot, what difference does it make? What does it matter if you have learned about the orbits of the planets, if you know the expanse of the oceans and the course of the stars, about the properties of plants and rocks and the secrets of nature? What difference does all of this make if you do not know yourself?[23] If, following Scripture, you have recognized the right path of arduous virtue, how has this helped you if madness leads you instead to a crooked, downward path? Suppose that you have learned by heart the deeds of illustrious heroes throughout the ages. What good is this if it does not change the way you live your daily life?

What shall I say about eloquence, except what you yourself will acknowledge, that you have often been deluded by your faith in it? And what does it matter that your listeners approve of your words if you yourself condemn them? For although the praise of those listening, which is not to be despised, seems to be the fruit of eloquence, if the praise of the orator himself is lacking, then how much pleasure can he really take in the clamoring of the multitude? For how can you delight others with your speech unless you have first delighted yourself? Clearly, you have often been disappointed in your quest for glory through eloquence, so that you easily understand how empty those vain things are in which you take such pride.

For what, I ask you, is more childish, what is crazier, than to ignore important things and to spend time on the study of words and, blind to your own faults, to take such pleasure in speech, just like certain small birds who, they say, are so delighted by the

---

[23]This passage echoes Augustine's *Confessions* X, 8, 15: "And men go to wonder at the heights of the mountains and the immense waves of the seas and the broad flow of rivers and the expanse of the ocean and the revolution of the stars and they abandon themselves." This is the passage that Petrarch reads at the summit of Mount Ventoux.

sweetness of their song that they sing themselves to death? Furthermore, it often happens in the course of your daily life that, much to your embarrassment, you are unable to express adequately in words things that you judge to be inferior to your eloquence. After all, how many things are there in nature for which we have no appropriate words? How many other things are there which have names yet whose full merit cannot be expressed by human eloquence before we actually experience them? How many times have I heard you complain, how many times have I seen your silent indignation, when neither tongue nor pen could express thoughts that existed easily and with the greatest clarity in your mind? Of what use, therefore, is this eloquence of yours, so narrow and fragile that it cannot embrace all things and cannot hold together what it has embraced?

You Latin speakers like to reproach the Greeks, and the Greeks you, for having too few words. Seneca judges them [the Greeks] to be richer in words. But Cicero, in the beginning of the work called *On the Ends of Good and Evil,* says, "I cannot but wonder where this insolent scorn for our own culture comes from. This is not the place for me to discuss it, but I feel it to be so and have often argued that the Latin language is not only not poorer, as most people think, but is indeed richer than Greek."[24] He often repeats this opinion, as in his *Tusculan Disputations,* when as he argues he exclaims, "O Greece, who think yourself so rich in words, how poor you really are!"[25] That man spoke this boldly, as one who knew that he was the prince of Latin eloquence and as one who at that time dared to provoke war with the Greeks over glory in this very art. Let me add here what Seneca—the same Seneca who so admired the Greeks—wrote in his *Declamations:* "Whatever Roman eloquence has to challenge or oppose to the insolence of the Greeks stems from Cicero."[26] High praise, but there is no doubt that it is true. There is, therefore, as you see, great controversy over leadership in

---

[24] Cicero, *On the Ends of Good and Evil* I, 3, 10.

[25] Cicero, *Tusculan Disputations* II, 15, 35.

[26] Seneca, *Controversies* I, 1, praef. 6. Petrarch thought that Seneca the rhetorician and Seneca the philosopher were the same person. In fact, there were two Senecas: Lucius (sometimes called Marcus) Annaeus Seneca (ca. 55 B.C.E.–39 C.E.), a rhetorician and author of the *Controversies,* which Petrarch knew only through a later summary and here calls the *Declamations,* and Lucius Annaeus Seneca (ca. 4 B.C.E.–65 C.E.), a philosopher (he wrote the *Moral Letters to Lucilius,* which Petrarch quotes frequently) and playwright.

eloquence, not just between us and the Greeks but also among even the most learned of us Latins. In our camp there are some who favor the Greeks, just as perhaps in theirs there are some who favor us, as some say Plutarch, the illustrious Greek philosopher, did. And then Seneca, one of us, although he deferred to Cicero because of the majesty of such sweet eloquence, in other things gave the crown to the Greeks. Cicero held the opposite opinion. If you want my view about these things, I say that both are right, both the one who called Greece poor in words and the one who called Italy poor in words. And if such disagreements occur in these two very famous regions, what hope is there for agreement in others?

Furthermore, when it comes to eloquence, consider this: How much faith can you have in your own abilities when you see that your whole country, of which you are a minuscule part, exhibits this poverty in speech? You will be ashamed at having wasted so much time on this thing that is impossible to attain and that would be utterly useless even if it were attained.

But let me move on from this to other important matters: Do you place value on the beauties of the body? "Do you not see the dangers that surround you?"[27] For what pleases you about your body? Perhaps your coloring or the gift of good health? Nothing is more fragile. Sudden fatigue from the most trivial of causes, the insult of various diseases, the bites of small worms, even the gentlest of breezes and many other such things can confound your good health. But perhaps you are deceived by the splendor of your physical appearance; perhaps the coloring and shape of your face give you something to wonder at, something to admire, something that pleases and delights you? Hasn't the story of Narcissus[28] terrified you? Hasn't courageous recognition of what you really are on the inside warned you of the vileness of the body? No. Content to focus on the appearance of the skin, you do not reach farther with your mind's eye. But even if all other arguments—and these are innumerable—were to cease, the sheer, disquieting passage of time, which takes something from us each and every day, ought to convince you beyond all question that the bloom of the body is fleeting and transient. Even if you think (but dare not say) that you yourself

[27]Virgil, *Aeneid* IV, 561.

[28]**Narcissus:** In Greek mythology, a beautiful boy whom the goddess Nemesis caused to fall in love with his own reflection. So great was his longing that eventually it consumed him.

are invincible in the face of time and disease and other changes in the form of the body, you at least ought to remember the ultimate end that destroys all things, and you ought to fix in your mind that line of Juvenal the satirist: "Only death truly reveals how meager are the bodies of men."[29] These are things that, in my opinion, prevent you, in your puffed-up arrogance, from considering the insignificance of your condition and from reflecting on the fact of your mortality. There are other causes as well, which I now aim to pursue.

Franciscus: Wait a minute, please. I fear that, crushed by the weight of these things, I will not be able to rise to respond.

Augustinus: Speak, please. Of course I will wait.

Franciscus: You have astonished and stunned me, throwing so much at me, accusing me of thoughts that I know never entered my mind. You say I trust in my intellect? I say the only evidence of my small intelligence is that I have never been able to trust in it. You think I take pride in the fact that I have read many books? If this reading has brought me some small modicum of learning, it has also brought many worries and cares. You claim that I pursue glory through the use of language, I who am angered at nothing more than the inadequacy of words to express my thoughts? Unless you are simply trying to provoke me, you know that I have always been conscious of my own smallness and that if I have ever thought I was worth something, this happened only in the face of another's ignorance. We are thus forced to accept, as I often say, that, in the well-known words of Cicero, we are made worthy not by our own virtue but by the frailty of others.[30]

And anyway, even if I possessed all those things that you describe—intellect, eloquence, good looks—what would these things bring me that was sufficiently magnificent to warrant pride and boasting? For I am neither so out of touch with myself nor so shallow as to allow myself to get excited over these fleeting ornaments. What good are intellect and knowledge and eloquence when they offer no remedy for the diseases that tear the soul apart? I remember lamenting this very thing at length in a letter I once wrote.[31] And what you say in that serious tone about the goods

[29]Juvenal, *Satires* 10, 172–73.
[30]Cicero, *On Obligations* II, 21, 75. Petrarch's citation is not exact.
[31]This perhaps refers to Petrarch, *Metrical Epistles* I, 6, 20–26.

associated with the body almost made me laugh. How could I possibly hope for anything from this mortal, corrupt body, when every day I feel it falling apart? May God spare me at least from that. I admit that when I was young, I took care to comb my hair and adorn my face, but this practice vanished with the years. Now I experience the very thing that the emperor Domitian described in a letter to a friend, writing about himself and complaining about the extraordinary transience of physical beauty: "Know that nothing is either as sweet or as fleeting as beauty."[32]

Augustinus: I could offer many arguments against these claims of yours. However, I prefer that your own conscience rather than my speeches induce shame in you. I won't pursue this matter, nor will I force the truth from you through torture. Instead, content as are noble avengers with a simple "you are wrong," I will ask that from now on, you avoid with all diligence those things that you contend have never afflicted you. If, for example, the loveliness of your features should begin to distract your soul, please remember what these bodily features will soon look like: how foul, how filthy, how they would horrify even you if you were to see them then. And repeat to yourself this philosophical saying: "I was born for something greater than to be a slave to my body."[33] For surely it is the height of idiocy that human beings neglect their true selves only to care assiduously for the body they inhabit. If a person were for a short time forced into a prison—dark, dank, disease-ridden—would he not, unless he were a complete fool, try to avoid all contact with the filthy walls and soil, and, hoping to get out soon, would he not attentively listen for the footsteps of his liberator? But if, having abandoned these thoughts, this man, drenched with the mud and the horrors of the prison, were afraid to leave and instead eagerly devoted all his energy to painting and decorating the very walls that confined him, thinking wrongly that he could somehow overcome the nature of that dank place, then would we not rightly think this man both wretched and insane?

This is how it is with you. You too know and love your prison. And just as you are about to be led or dragged from there, you cling to it, working to adorn what you ought to despise. But it should be like what you had the father of the great Scipio say in your poem *Africa:* "We hate and dread the snares and chains that

[32]Suetonius, *Lives of the Caesars,* "Domitian," 18.
[33]Seneca, *Moral Letters to Lucilius* 65, 21.

we long knew as obstacles to freedom; what we are now, we love."[34] It is certainly amazing that you make others say what you ought to say to yourself! But, moving on, I cannot overlook that one word in your speech which perhaps seems most humble to you but strikes me as the height of arrogance.

Franciscus: I am sorry if I said something in a prideful way. But if the soul is the moderator of words and deeds, then my own attests that I said nothing arrogant.

Augustinus: Certainly, it is a much more intolerable kind of pride to denigrate others than it is to excessively exalt oneself; and I would much prefer that you praise everyone else, although putting yourself above them, than that, having stepped on all others, you arrogantly take up a shield of humility out of contempt for someone else.

Franciscus: Take my words however you will. As for me, I attribute little either to myself or to others. I am ashamed to say what experience has made me think of the majority of humankind.

Augustinus: To despise yourself is very prudent, but it is most dangerous and vain to despise others. However, let's move on. Do you know what else turns you from the right path?

Franciscus: Tell me, whatever it is, only please don't accuse me of envy.

Augustinus: If only pride had harmed you as little as envy! It seems to me that you are free from this failing. But I am ready to talk about others.

Franciscus: You will not undo me with any of these accusations. Be frank. Tell me what it is that turns me astray.

Augustinus: A desire for temporal things.

Franciscus: Come on, you can't be serious! I have never heard anything so ridiculous!

Augustinus: How quickly indeed you fall apart—you forget your own promise! And I made no mention at all of envy.

Franciscus: But you accuse me of greed? I know of no one less affected by greed than myself.

Augustinus: Say what you like in your own defense, but believe me, this failing is not as foreign to you as you think.

Franciscus: I am not free from the stain of ambition?

Augustinus: Not even from ambition.

---

[34] Petrarch, *Africa* I, 329–30.

Franciscus: Well, keep going. Don't stop now. Repeat the charges; fulfill your obligation as accuser. I am ready for whatever new wounds
you plan to inflict.

Augustinus: You have described as *accusations* and *wounds* what is in
fact the truth. The satirist was right: "The accuser will be the one
who speaks the truth."[35] So too was the comic poet, who said, "Flattery makes friends, the truth makes hatred."[36]

But tell me, what is the value of all these worries and preoccupations that eat at your soul? What is the point in such a short life of
weaving long-term hopes? "The shortness of life forbids that we
plan for distant dreams."[37] You're always reading this, yet you
ignore it. You will answer, I think, that you are compelled to distant
dreams out of love for your friends, and so you find a nice excuse
for your error. But really, how demented it is that in order to be a
friend to another, you declare war and enmity against yourself!

Franciscus: I am not so miserly and inhuman as to be unaffected by
concern for friends, especially those whose virtue and merit draws
me to them. These are the ones I admire and respect, the ones I
love and feel compassion for. At the same time, however, I am not
so generous that I would sacrifice myself completely for the sake of
my friends. I can't say I would do that. I do want to fashion a daily
life for myself, and I also want this (because you assaulted me with
spears from Horace, I will protect myself with a Horatian shield):
"Let there be a supply of books and provisions to last one year, so
that I am not anxious, uncertain about what time may bring."[38] And
because I also plan, as the same poet says, "to pass my old age neither in laziness nor without the songs of the poets,"[39] and because I
very much dread the snares of a drawn-out life, I have long provided for these two things, and to the study of literature I add
domestic concerns and duties. But I do these latter so lazily that I
clearly take them up only when forced.

Augustinus: I see now how deeply into your heart such silly ideas,
your excuses for your folly, have penetrated. But why do these
words of the satirist not dwell equally deeply within you? "But by
what cruel fate is such wealth painstakingly gathered up, when
surely it is madness, a sign of obvious dementia, to live in desperate

---

[35] Juvenal, *Satires* 1, 161.
[36] Terence, *Andria* I, 1, 68.
[37] Horace, *Poems* I, 4, 15.
[38] Horace, *Letters* I, 18, 109–10.
[39] Horace, *Poems* I, 31, 19–20.

poverty in order to die rich?"[40] I guess it is because you think it a splendid thing to die wrapped in a purple shroud, to be buried in a marble tomb, and to leave the battle over your impressive estate to your heirs. And so you desire the wealth through which these other things can be accomplished. This labor is pointless and, as far as I am concerned, also crazy. If you consider common human nature, you see that it is content with little. As for your own nature, unless common misconceptions impede your judgment, you see that scarcely anyone has ever been born for whom less sufficed. The poet was thinking of common habits or perhaps of his own when he said, "The earth gives only pitiful food, the trees hard fruit; the grass from plucked out roots feeds me."[41]

You, on the other hand, must acknowledge that for yourself, there is nothing sweeter or more appealing than such simple food—that is, if you follow your own judgment rather than that of the demented crowd. Why, then, do you torment yourself? If you measure your life by your own standards, you have been rich for a long time. If you accept the standards of the majority, you can never be rich. Something will always be missing, and as you strive to attain it, you will be taken over by the dangerous ways of desire. Do you remember how you used to wander with delight through the remote countryside? On some occasions, you would listen attentively to the murmur of the rushing spring water as you lay on a grassy green bed. At other times, you would sit on the open, high hilltops, and freely survey the land stretched out below; or, finding a shady spot in the midst of a sun-drenched valley and overtaken by sweet sleep, you would delight in the welcome virtues of silence. Never lazy, always thinking about important things, and, with only the Muses for companions, never alone. In short, you were like the old man Virgil wrote about: "In his own mind his wealth matched that of kings and, returning to his house late at night, he filled his table with plentiful and home-grown food."[42] You too, returning at sunset to your simple home and content with your possessions, did you not then think yourself by far the richest and happiest of mortals?

Franciscus: Yes, yes, of course I remember, and the memory of that time fills me with longing and regret.

[40] Juvenal, *Satires* 14, 135–37.
[41] Virgil, *Aeneid* III, 649–50.
[42] Virgil, *Georgics* IV, 132–33.

Augustinus: Why do you of all people mourn? Who was it, after all, who brought about all these evils that you now suffer? It was your own soul, which was ashamed to obey the laws of its own nature and believed itself a slave because it would not break its chains. Now this violent soul has taken off with you, and unless you rein it in, it will hurl you to your death. Ever since you first began to disdain the berries growing on your branches, ever since simple clothes and the company of simple people became contemptible in your eyes, you, driven by greed, have returned to the tumult of city life. And I can tell from your words and demeanor just how happy and peaceful a life this is for you.

What miseries have you not seen there? How can you remain so stubborn in the face of your own unhappy experience? You still hesitate, perhaps caught in the snare of sin, so that, with God's approval, you who spent your childhood there under the discipline of another might similarly now, as your own master, waste away your old age. I remember when you were still young and no greed, no ambition touched you, when you held out the promise of becoming a great man. Now, unhappy creature, your ways have changed, and the closer you get to the end of your life, the more painstakingly you accumulate provisions for the rest of the way. What is left, then, except that on the day of your death, which may be imminent but in any event cannot be far off, you sit half alive, panting after gold and measuring your wealth? For whatever grows with each passing day must necessarily be at its maximum size on the last day.

Franciscus: If in anticipation of the poverty of old age, I should procure some support for that weary time of life, what is so bad about that?

Augustinus: How ridiculous and negligent it is to worry so about a time that may never come, and one that in any case you will endure for only the briefest moment, while you forget the state in which you will find yourself and from which there is no escape once you have arrived there. But that is your hateful habit: You care about transitory things; you neglect the eternal. And in your error, which leads you to seek a shield against the poverty of old age, I think that that phrase of Virgil's possesses you: "the ant, fearing a poor old age."[43] And so you have chosen this ant as your teacher in life, excusable, perhaps, through the words of the satirist: "Finally, with

---

[43]Ibid., I, 186.

the ant as teacher, some feared cold and hunger."[44] But unless you have transformed yourself completely according to the ways of ants, you will find that nothing is more miserable, nothing more bitter, than always to suffer poverty lest one day you be poor.

So what am I saying? Am I urging you to be poor? Not, certainly, to seek this condition, but rather to tolerate it with effort if Fortune, who wreaks havoc in human affairs, compels it. In fact, I think that in every situation, one should seek the middle path. I do not, therefore, remind you of the rule of those who say, "Bread and water suffice for human life; no one who has these is poor, and whoever has confined his desire to these things will rival Jove in happiness."[45] No, I do not limit human life to only "grain and river water."[46] Such advice is as arrogant as it is inappropriate and hateful to human ears. And so, that I might treat your sickness, I advise not that you purge yourself of natural desire, but that you rein it in. What you own would have been enough to meet your needs if you yourself had been capable of satisfying them. But as it is, what poverty you now suffer you yourself created. The accumulation of wealth also amasses cares and anxiety. This has been discussed so often that no argument is needed here. What extraordinary error and pathetic blindness it is for the human soul—whose nature is so noble and whose origins are divine—to ignore divine things and to gape with longing at the meager quarry of this earth. Think, I beg you, and exert the eyes of your mind, and do not let the shining glitter of gold impede their vision. Every time you are dragged by the hooks of avarice and diverted from the highest course to these things below, do you not think that you have fallen, hurled from the sky to the earth, and that you have been plunged out of the stars into the deepest abyss?

Franciscus: Yes, I do think that, and I cannot begin to say how much damage I sustain when I fall.

Augustinus: Why, then, are you not afraid of something that you have so often experienced? And when you are lifted up to higher things, why don't you hold on more tenaciously?

Franciscus: I do try, but because the necessity of the human condition shakes me, I am pulled down against my will. For I suspect that it

---

[44]Juvenal, *Satires* 6, 360–61.

[45]Seneca, *Moral Letters to Lucilius* 25, 4. **Jove:** Another name for Jupiter, the chief god in Roman mythology.

[46]Lucan, *Pharsalia* IV, 381.

was not without reason that the ancient poets dedicated the twin peaks of Parnassus to two gods. They did this so that from Apollo, whom they called the god of the intellect, they could ask for internal presence of mind, and from Bacchus they could ask for a sufficient supply of external goods. Not only the teaching of experience suggests this twofold worship but also the authority of the most learned men, whom I certainly do not have to parade before you, of all people. And so, although the *number* of ancient gods is completely ridiculous, nonetheless the idea behind the practice of those poets is hardly irrational. As for me, I offer a similar prayer to the one true god from whom all help comes. I don't think I am being crazy, unless it seems otherwise to you.

Augustinus: I don't deny that your view makes sense. However, I disapprove of how inappropriately you allocate your time. You used to devote all your time and energy to higher, ethical matters, and whatever time you were forced to spend on other things you considered wasted. But now you allocate to noble things only as much time as your greedy desire leaves left over. Who would not like to arrive at an old age in which he alternates the advice of men in this way? But what limit would you accept, what measure? Set a goal for yourself; when you arrive at it, you can stop and rest awhile. You know the force of the saying that, though it came from a human mouth, has the force of an oracle: "A greedy man is always in need; seek a fixed limit to your longing."[47] So, then, what limit will there be to your desires?

Franciscus: Neither to be in need nor to have too much, neither to command nor to submit to others.

Augustinus: You must shed your humanity and become a god if you are never to be in need. Or maybe you did not know that of all animals, human beings are the most needy.

Franciscus: I have heard that very often but would like my memory refreshed.

Augustinus: Just look at this human—naked and unformed, born crying and wailing, seeking the comfort of a few drops of milk, trembling and crawling, in need of the help of another; this creature whom mute animals feed and clothe, possessing a frail and mortal body, a restless spirit, besieged by all kinds of diseases, subject to countless passions, in need of advice, happy one minute, sad the next; weak-willed, not knowing how to restrain his desires, ignorant

[47] Horace, *Letters* I, 2, 56.

of what things in what quantity are good for him, unable to regulate his desire for food and drink. For this creature, provisions for the body, something that all other animals find easily at hand, must be procured through much labor. See him puffy from sleep, stuffed with food, stupefied by drink, weary from staying awake, racked with hunger, parched from thirst; a creature both greedy and timid, bored with what he has, mourning what he has lost, anxious simultaneously about the past, the present, and the future. Arrogant amidst his miseries, conscious of his frailty, inferior to the vilest worm, his life is short and its course uncertain, but his ultimate fate is inevitable, open as he is to a thousand different ways of death.

Franciscus: You have so heaped up our miseries and wants that I am almost sorry I was born a human being!

Augustinus: And yet in this human condition of such weakness and destitution, you continue to expect a degree of wealth and power that no king or emperor has ever enjoyed.

Franciscus: Who used those words? Who said anything about wealth or power?

Augustinus: But what greater wealth is there than not to be in need? And what greater power is there than not to submit to others? For certainly the kings and lords of the earth whom you think the wealthiest need countless things. And the leaders of armies actually depend on those they seem to command, and surrounded by the armed legions who make them feared, they in turn become afraid. So stop hoping for the impossible. Instead, accept your fate as a human being. Learn how to live both in abundance and in need; learn how to command and also to submit. Do not imagine that by living according to your own rules, you can shake off the yoke of fortune that binds the necks even of kings. You will know that you have finally cut off this yoke when, having scorned human passions, you have submitted wholly to the rule of virtue. From then on you will be free, needing nothing, subject to no human being— at last a king both truly powerful and completely happy.

Franciscus: Now I despise my earlier undertaking, and I desire to desire nothing. But I am a captive to perverse habit, and I always feel an unsatisfied yearning deep in my heart.

Augustinus: That yearning is—to return to our subject—exactly what keeps you from the contemplation of death. While entangled in earthly worries, you do not lift your eyes to higher things. If you trust my advice, you will cast down these worries as if they were deadly burdens on the soul. To cast them down would not be hard, if only you would conform yourself according to your own nature and allow yourself to be ruled and guided by it rather than by the violent passions of the crowd.

Franciscus: I will and want to do that. But I would like to hear at last what you started to say earlier about ambition.

Augustinus: Why do you ask me to do what you can do for yourself? Look into your heart. You will find that among your other afflictions, ambition holds a significant place.

Franciscus: So I gained nothing by fleeing city life whenever possible, nor by scorning public life, nor by seeking the deep woods and quiet countryside, nor by expressing my hatred for vain honors? With all this, still I am accused of ambition!

Augustinus: You mortals give up many things not because you despise them, but rather because you despair of ever being able to acquire them. For hope and desire inflame each other, so that when one grows cold, the other dies away, and when one heats up, the other boils over.

Franciscus: What, I ask you, was to keep me from hoping? Was I lacking all accomplishment?

Augustinus: I am not talking about the accomplishments you possessed, but certainly you lacked those through which people get ahead in the world today: cultivating the support of the powerful, flattering, cheating, promising, lying, posturing, deceiving, putting up with all kinds of insults and humiliations. Bereft of these and other such arts, and having realized that your nature would not be conquered, you turned to other preoccupations. You acted cautiously and wisely. For, as Cicero says, "to fight with the gods as the giants did, this is to war against nature itself."[48]

Franciscus: Farewell to the honors bestowed by the powerful, if they are acquired through arts such as these.

Augustinus: Well said. But you have not yet proved your innocence to me, for you do not suggest that you have ceased to desire these honors, but rather that you recoil from the trouble of pursuing them. You are like the person who, fearing the effort of travel, retreats from the journey, insisting that Rome is not worth seeing anyway. You have not actually retreated from the pursuit of honors, as you are persuading yourself and as you are trying to persuade me. Don't bury your head in the sand. Whatever you think, whatever you do, I see. And the fact that you boast of your flight from

---

[48]Cicero, *On Old Age* 2, 5.

city life and of your desire for the quiet country indicates not your release from, but rather a change in, culpability.

Many roads lead to the same end. And believe me, although you have deserted the path worn by the feet of the crowd, you still struggle with the very ambition that you say you have rejected. But you do so in a less direct way. For you, leisure, solitude, utter indifference to human affairs, and your precious studies lead to ambition, and the end of these pursuits is glory.

Franciscus: You are pushing me into a corner, but one from which I think I can escape. However, because time is short and it must be allocated among many things, let's move on, if you agree, to other topics.

Augustinus: Follow me, then, as I proceed. We need not mention gluttony, to which you are not inclined, although sometimes, as you indulge the tastes of your friends, an uncharacteristically sumptuous meal graces your table. Still, I fear nothing for you from gluttony. As soon as the country reclaims you as a resident, snatches you from the city, all the dangers of such pleasures immediately disappear. And at that point, once city things are no longer present, I see you living in such a way that I delight in your modesty and temperance, extraordinary for your time or indeed for any time.

I pass over anger too. Although sometimes it does inflame you more than it should, nonetheless you are, by virtue of the goodness of your nature, usually quick to restrain your emotions, mindful of the advice of Horace: "Anger is a kind of fleeting madness; control your passion, for unless it obeys, it rules. Restrain this passion with fetters, bind it up with chains."[49]

Franciscus: I acknowledge that this saying of Horace and other similar advice given by the philosophers has helped me a little, but above all what has helped me is the recollection of how short life is. For what madness it is to pass the few precious days we have among our fellow human beings in hating and hurting them! For surely the day is coming that will extinguish these flames of passion in human breasts and put an end to all hatred. If we want for our enemy nothing more serious than death, then our most evil wish will assuredly be granted. And so why contribute to one's own or another's ruin? Why waste the best part of a life that is all too short? Why take days, which even when allocated with the greatest economy, scarcely suffice either for the enjoyment of honest pleasures or for

---

[49]Horace, *Letters* I, 2, 62–63. Horace has *frenis* (bridles) for *vinclis* (fetters).

the planning of the future? Why take such scarce days from their necessary and appropriate uses and turn them to sadness and death for ourselves or others? To this point, this awareness of the shortness of life has in truth so helped me that I have not been completely conquered by the impulse to anger, and if I did fall, I recovered. Yet no teaching or technique has yet freed me completely from gusts of anger.

Augustinus: But since I do not fear from such gusts of anger a shipwreck for you or others, I can live with the fact that though you do not strive to meet the expectations of the Stoics, who promise to completely root out diseases from the soul, you are content in this matter of anger with the milder techniques of the Peripatetics.[50] Leaving these matters aside for now, let us move quickly on to more dangerous temptations against which you must especially protect yourself.

Franciscus: Good God, what could possibly be more dangerous than what we have already discussed?

Augustinus: Well, to what degree have you been consumed by the flames of lust?

Franciscus: Enough so that I have at times lamented that I was not born without feeling. I would prefer to be an insensate stone than to be undone by so many impulses in my body.

Augustinus: There you have it, the thing that most drives you away from all meditation on divine things. For what does the heavenly teaching of Plato demonstrate if not that the soul must be kept away from bodily desires and that images of earthly things must be eradicated so that the soul can rise, pure and free, to examine the mysteries of the divine, to which it joins a contemplation of its own mortality? You recognize what I am saying, and these ideas from Plato's books are known and familiar to you. Indeed, you are said to have recently devoted yourself most eagerly to the study of these books.

Franciscus: I did devote myself to them, I confess, eagerly and with great anticipation. But the newness of a foreign language and the sudden departure of my teacher cut short my plan.[51] Still, the ideas

---

[50]**Peripatetics:** Followers of Aristotle. As Petrarch presents them, the Stoics argued that the perfectly virtuous soul could not be disturbed by any external stimulus or emotion, whereas the Peripatetics understood emotion as something to be regulated (rather than completely controlled) by virtue.

[51]In the summer of 1342, Petrarch began to study Greek with a monk named Barlaam, but this work ended when Barlaam was made a bishop.

that you speak of are very familiar to me from your writings and the work of other Platonists.

Augustinus: It hardly matters from whom you learned the truth, although a respected authority can be of great benefit.

Franciscus: As for me, I certainly respect Plato's authority, the man of whom Cicero, in his *Tusculan Disputations,* wrote the following words, which I carry deep within myself: "Plato," Cicero says, "even if he were to offer no rational argument (you see what respect I accord him), would conquer me simply by virtue of the authority of his name."[52] Furthermore, as for me, when I think of that man's divine intellect, it would seem unjust if Plato were obliged to produce proof and argument when the herd of Pythagoreans absolve their leader from such obligations.[53] But, to get back to the point, authority, reason, and experience have for a long time so commended this idea of Plato's to me[54] that I believe nothing more true or more holy could be said. And so at times, with the hand of God supporting me, I was able to raise myself up so that I recognized, with great and incredible delight, what was then helping me and what had injured me in the past. And now, when I have relapsed again by my own weight into my former misery, I contend, with great bitterness, in my mind with what has once more caused me to fall. I tell you this so that you will not be surprised when I claim to have direct experience of Plato's teaching.

Augustinus: Certainly, I am not surprised! I was there through your ordeal. I saw you both rise and fall, and now, taking pity on you, I have resolved to bring you help.

Franciscus: I am grateful for your compassion, but what kind of human help is there for me?

Augustinus: None. But there is much divine help. No one can restrain the passions unless God has given this capacity to him.[55] Thus this gift of moderation must first of all be sought from him, and it must

[52]Cicero, *Tusculan Disputations* I, 21, 49. Petrarch's quotation differs slightly from what is now the standard Cicero text.

[53]Petrarch is relying on a distinction between an Ionian (or Greek) philosophical tradition that began with an interest in understanding the composition of the world and the cosmos, and an Italian (or Pythagorean) philosophical tradition that began with an emphasis on the intuitive grasp of truths among an initiated group. See Augustine, *The City of God* VIII, 2.

[54]Franciscus is referring to the ideas described by Augustinus regarding the need to isolate the soul from bodily desires and from the products of the imagination.

[55]An allusion to Wisdom 8:21 and Augustine, *Confessions* VI, 11, 20.

be sought with humility and often with tears. He does not often deny things that are right for us to seek.

Franciscus: I have beseeched him so often that I fear God finds me a pest.

Augustinus: But you haven't done it with appropriate humility or gravity. You have always reserved some small place inside for future desires. You have asked that your prayers be granted, but in the future. I speak from experience, for the same thing happened to me. I would say, "Give me chastity, but not now; wait a little while, the time will soon come. Let this vigorous time of life take its course, follow its own laws. It would be worse to return later to these youthful things. Let me therefore give up these things when my age makes me less inclined to such habits and when past indulgence of desire has removed the fear of a relapse."[56] Do you not see, as you say such things, that you pray for one thing yet long for another?

Franciscus: How so?

Augustinus: Because to ask for something in the future is to neglect it in the present.

Franciscus: I have with tears often asked for it in the present, hoping that after the chains of desire had been broken and after the miseries of this life had been overcome, I would emerge safe, and out of these many storms of useless worries I would swim away as if into some safe port. But in spite of this, you know how many shipwrecks I have suffered among the same rocks, and how many, if left to my own resources, I would suffer in the future.

Augustinus: Trust me, something was always missing when you were praying. Otherwise, the supreme Giver would have granted your prayer, or, as was the case with the apostle Paul, he would have denied it, only to allow you to undergo the experience of your infirmity and to attain to perfection of virtue.

Franciscus: I believe that. I will pray with more ardor. I will not tire, I will not be ashamed, and I will not despair. Perhaps the all-powerful one will, out of compassion for my suffering, adapt his ear to my daily prayers, and if he would not have denied them had they been worthy, he will make them worthy.

Augustinus: A wise plan! Keep trying; and as is the habit of those lying on the ground, raise yourself up on your elbow and look around for imminent dangers, so that you are not torn apart by sudden attacks

[56]Petrarch is alluding to Augustine, *Confessions* VI, 11, 19.

as you lie there. Meanwhile, do not grow lazy in imploring help from the one able to lift you up. He will perhaps come to you just when you think he is far away. Always keep in mind that idea of Plato's that deserves never to be forgotten: Nothing presents a greater obstacle to recognition of the divine than carnal appetites and burning desire. Reflect ever diligently on this idea. This is the best advice I can give you.

Franciscus: So that you might understand how deeply I revere this doctrine, I have warmly embraced it not only when I find it at home, in its own context,[57] but also when it is hidden in the works of other writers. Wherever I saw this idea expressed, I noted it in my heart.

Augustinus: Go on—what exactly do you mean?

Franciscus: You know Virgil. You remember how many dangers he led his hero through on that horrible last night of the Trojan War, when the city of Troy fell?

Augustinus: I know. What is more commonly discussed in every school? Virgil has his hero recount his experiences in these words: "Who could describe the devastation of that night? Who could describe the bodies, or cry tears equal to our pain? The ancient city, for so long the ruler of many, is destroyed. Thousands upon thousands lie dead, bodies in the street, corpses in our homes and on the thresholds of our temples. And not only Trojans spill their blood that night. Once courage returns to the hearts of the conquered, the victorious Greeks too fall dead; everywhere there is heartless grief, everywhere terror and imminent death."[58]

Franciscus: But as long as Venus accompanied Aeneas as he wandered through enemy armies in his ruined city, he could not discover, even though his eyes were open, the anger of the offended gods. And as long as Venus was speaking to him, he could think only of things of this earth. But recall what happened after she left him. He soon saw the angry faces of the gods, and he recognized the dangers all around him: "The ominous faces of the gods appear, with the great divine enmity for Troy."[59] From this passage, I

---

[57]That is, in the writings of Plato himself.

[58]Virgil, *Aeneid* II, 361–69. Petrarch's quotation is not exact.

[59]Ibid., II, 622–23. At this point in the *Aeneid,* the Greeks are destroying the city of Troy, and Aeneas, a leader of the Trojans, comes upon Helen, whom he blames for causing the war. As Aeneas lunges in anger at Helen, his mother, the goddess Venus, appears and holds him back. Helen is not to blame, says Venus; this is the will of the gods. Look, she says, and I'll show you. As she disappears, "the ominous faces of the gods appear."

conclude that association with Venus takes away the capacity to see the divine.

Augustinus: Assuredly, with this interpretation you have discovered light amidst the clouds. For this is how truth dwells in poetic creations: It must be brought out into the light from the dark corners. But because we must return again to the subject of this passion, let us leave the rest of our discussion until that later time.

Franciscus: So that I might know where you are leading me, may I ask why you intend to return to this?

Augustinus: I have not yet touched on the deepest wounds of your mind, and I think we should talk about them last, so that the topic we discuss at the end will cling to your memory. Though we have briefly discussed this second carnal appetite, we will have much more to say.

Franciscus: Go ahead then.

Augustinus: Unless you are tenaciously stubborn, there remains, at last, no controversy between us.

Franciscus: Nothing could make me happier than to banish all contention from the world. For nothing has ever seemed so clear to me that I have willingly argued about it. Even an argument among friends possesses a certain bitterness that is hostile and contrary to the ways of friendship. But move on, please, to the matters about which you think we will now agree.

Augustinus: A deadly plague afflicts your soul, which moderns call *accidia* and the ancients called *aegritudo.*[60]

Franciscus: The very name of the disease makes me shudder.

Augustinus: I am not surprised. You have suffered severely from it for a long time.

Franciscus: I know. With almost all other afflictions that I suffer, there comes some sense of sweetness, albeit a false one. With this one, however, everything is sad, hard, miserable, and horrific. The road to despair beckons relentlessly, and everything colludes to push unhappy souls to self-destruction. And whereas I experience the rest of the passions in frequent but fleeting attacks, this plague holds me so tenaciously that for days on end it tortures me. When this happens, my days seem to have no light or life. All is dark as

[60]By "moderns," Petrarch means his contemporaries. *Accidia,* which suggests melancholy, hopelessness, and apathy, is an important concept in much of Petrarch's work and a feeling from which he repeatedly suffers.

night and bitter as death. And (the great culmination of my miseries) I so feed on the tears and the suffering, deriving from them some kind of dark pleasure, that I must be torn from my misery against my will.

Augustinus: You know your sickness well. Now you must recognize its cause. So tell me, what is it that makes you so sad? The inevitable passage of time? Some disease of the body? Some injury done by heartless Fortune?

Franciscus: No single thing alone would be able to do this to me. If I were challenged to a single battle, I would stand my ground. As it is, I am attacked from all sides.

Augustinus: Tell me more specifically what attacks you.

Franciscus: Each time I suffer an injury of Fortune, I stand firm and undaunted. I remind myself that often, even when seriously wounded, I have come away from such contests the victor. But if soon after this injury another injury strikes, I begin to stagger a little. And if after these two injuries a third and a fourth should follow, I am forced to escape, not in a hasty retreat, but step by step, to the citadel of reason. If even there Fortune continues to press in on me with her whole army, and if, in an effort to subdue me, she heaps up before me the miseries of the human condition and the memory of my past sorrow and the fear of sorrow to come, then, cornered, hemmed in on all sides, horrified at such a collection of evils, I begin to groan, terrified. This is how my disease is born. I am like someone surrounded by countless enemies who has no way to escape. There is no hope of mercy or solace. Instead, with weapons aimed at me, with trenches dug, everything threatens destruction. Already the turrets of my citadel tremble, the ladders scale the ramparts, the hooks are fastened to the walls, and flames engulf the foundation. Seeing the flashing swords and the threatening faces of the enemy, realizing that death was at hand, who would not shake with fear, who would not grieve, since even if these immediate threats go away, the loss of liberty itself is the greatest sadness to strong men?

Augustinus: Although you have told this story a bit haphazardly, I see that the cause of all your troubles is a single perverse opinion that has overcome and continues to overcome innumerable people. Do you think yourself bad?

Franciscus: The worst.

Augustinus: Why?

Franciscus: Lots of reasons.

Augustinus: You are like those who at the slightest offense relive every grudge they have ever felt.

Franciscus: No wound on me now is so old that forgetting has erased it. The injuries that torture me now are all recent. And if any of them were able to be alleviated by time, Fortune struck the same place again so quickly that no wound has ever completely scarred over. And when this is added to my hatred and contempt for the human condition generally, I am not strong enough to overcome my intense anguish. It doesn't matter to me whether you call this *aegritudo* or *accidia* or some other name. We agree about what it is.

Augustinus: Because, as I see now, your disease is sustained by deep roots, it will not be enough to treat just the surface. If we do that, the disease will quickly return. Instead, we must dig it out entirely. I am not even sure where to start, so many things are involved. But in order to go at this task logically, I will discuss each aspect of the problem separately. Tell me, what do you think disturbs you the most?

Franciscus: Everything I see or hear or feel.

Augustinus: Come now. Nothing at all pleases you?

Franciscus: Nothing or almost nothing.

Augustinus: I wish that at least the better things in life gave you pleasure! But what is most displeasing? Please try to answer.

Franciscus: I already answered.

Augustinus: This is a symptom of what I called *accidia*. Everything about yourself and your life displeases you.

Franciscus: And everything about others and their lives too.

Augustinus: This feeling has the same cause. But we have to start somewhere. Are you really as displeasing to yourself as you say?

Franciscus: Stop plaguing me with your bothersome questions! Words cannot express my displeasure with myself.

Augustinus: So even the things that others envy you find repulsive.

Franciscus: Whoever envies this pitiful wretch must himself be most pitiful indeed!

Augustinus: What of everything most displeases you?

Franciscus: I don't know.

Augustinus: If I guess right, will you tell me?

Franciscus: Yes, of course.

Augustinus: You are angry at Fortune.

Franciscus: Why shouldn't I hate Fortune—Fortune who is proud, violent, blind, who deranges human affairs on a whim?

Augustinus: Everyone complains about these common conditions. Let's move on to injuries that specifically afflict you. What if your complaints are unjust? Would you not then wish to make peace with yourself?

Franciscus: It will be hard to persuade me of that. But if you were to prove my complaints unjust, then I would yield.

Augustinus: You think that Fortune has dealt with you in a stingy way?

Franciscus: Not in a stingy way. Rather most greedily, most unjustly, most arrogantly, most cruelly.

Augustinus: If we judge by comedic theater, there is not one character called "the Whiner," there are many. To this point, you have been one of this crowd. I would prefer that you belong to more select company. Anyway, since this matter is so familiar that hardly anything new can be said about it, will you accept an old remedy for an old disease?

Franciscus: Whatever you think.

Augustinus: All right then. Has poverty forced you to endure hunger or thirst or cold?

Franciscus: Fortune has not yet been that harsh.

Augustinus: Yet how many experience these hardships every day!

Franciscus: Try a different remedy, if you can, for this one does not help at all. I am not one of those who in their own miseries take pleasure in a surrounding army of lamenting, sobbing people who are also miserable. Nor do I cry less over the sorrows of others than over my own.

Augustinus: I do not expect that the sufferings of others will delight you, but rather that they will offer you some consolation and teach you, seeing the fortunes of others, to be content with yours. Not everyone can be in first place. For if no one were in second, how could there be a first? Things are going well for you mortals if you have not been thrown into dire straits and if, out of so many vicious whims of Fortune, you have suffered only mild ones. It is true that one must offer more potent remedies to those who have suffered extreme calamities. You, however, do not need these at this time, for you have been wounded by Fortune less severely.

This is, indeed, what gets you humans into such desperate situations: Each one, oblivious to his own actual fate, pursues in his own mind the highest place. But because, as I said, not everyone can attain it, outrage rises up in those who fail. If only humans knew the miseries that accompanied the highest place, they would recoil from what they so eagerly desire. This we know from the testimony of those who have climbed with incredible effort to the highest summit of things and whom nonetheless we see cursing the too easy gratification of their hopes. This truth, which should be familiar to everyone, should be especially known to you, to whom long experience has shown how high rank brings unhappiness, anxiety, and misery. And so it happens that no station in life is without its complaints, as both the winners and the losers feel just cause for lamenting. The former think that they have been deceived, the latter that they have been neglected. Therefore, follow Seneca's advice: "When you see how many are in front of you, think of how many follow you. If you wish to make peace with God and with your lot in life, think how many you have surpassed."[61] And, as the same author says in the same text, "set a bound which you cannot go beyond even if you should want to."[62]

Franciscus: A long time ago, I set a bound to my desires, a clear one and, unless I am mistaken, a very modest one. But what place is there for modesty among the arrogant and shameless ways of these times? Now they call it laziness and stupidity.

Augustinus: So the name-calling of the crowd is able to disrupt your state of mind? The crowd, which never judges accurately and never calls things by their right names? Didn't you used to despise vulgar opinion?

Franciscus: I have never had greater scorn for it, believe me. I care no more what the crowd thinks of me than I do a herd of brute animals.

Augustinus: So, then, what is the problem?

Franciscus: It bothers me that although none of my contemporaries has desired more modestly than I, none has had more difficulty in achieving their desires. I have never sought after the highest place. Truth, our witness and witness to everything, knows. She who always sees my thoughts knows how often I have gone over in my mind, as humans do, all the positions and ranks in life. I have never thought that the tranquillity and serenity of mind, which are in my view to be sought above all else, lay in the highest position that Fortune can bestow. And so, horrified by a life filled with anxiety and worries, I have exercised clear judgment and preferred some middle position. I have approved—not only in words but also in my

---

[61]Seneca, *Moral Letters to Lucilius* 15, 10. Seneca has *deos* (gods) for Petrarch's *deum* (God).

[62]Ibid., 11.

heart—of this passage from Horace: "Whoever loves the golden mean is safely free from the squalor of a crumbling roof and wisely lacks an enviable palace."[63] And Horace's reason for saying this pleases me as much as his words: "The taller pine is more often tattered by the wind, the lofty turrets fall hardest, and lightning strikes the highest mountains."[64] I regret that I have never achieved this mean.

Augustinus: What if this middle place, this golden mean, is actually behind you? What if you have achieved the true middle place a long time ago, and achieved it easily? What if, in fact, you left the middle place far behind a long time ago, and now, in your current place, you show cause for many more to envy than to despise you?

Franciscus: Even if *they* think that, *I* don't.

Augustinus: This perverse opinion is without doubt the cause of all your troubles, but especially of the *aegritudo,* the despair, that you feel. As Cicero says, "You must flee this Charybdis using every oar and every sail."[65]

Franciscus: From what am I supposed to flee? In what direction should I point my bow? What would you have me believe, except what I see before my own eyes?

Augustinus: You see where you have turned your eyes. If you look behind you, you will see that countless follow you and that you are somewhat closer to the front of the line than to the rear. But your pride and your stubbornness do not let you turn around.

Franciscus: But I *have* looked back from time to time, and I *have* thought about the many that come behind me; nor am I ashamed of my fate. Rather, I am annoyed and troubled by all these worries. It's as if—to use Horace's words again—"I am drifting along uncertain of what will happen from day to day."[66] If this anxiety would go away, the possessions I have would be more than enough, and I would gladly say what Horace says in the same poem: "Friend, what do you think I pray for? That I have what I have now, or even less. And that I live the time remaining to me for myself, if indeed the gods grant me any more time."[67] But as I am always anxious

[63] Horace, *Poems* II, 10, 5–8.

[64] Ibid., 9–12.

[65] Cicero, *Tusculan Dispuations* III, 11, 25. **Charybdis:** One of two large rocks (the other is called Scylla) between the Italian peninsula and Sicily; also, the frightening creature that lives there.

[66] Horace, *Letters* I, 18, 110.

[67] Ibid., 106–8.

about the future, always worried and uncertain, I take no pleasure from the gifts of Fortune. And up until now, as you see, I have been dependent on others to live, which is the most wretched state of all. I pray that during my old age, I who lived most of my life in such stormy waters may come into port to die.

Augustinus: Ah, so you—in the great whirlwind of human affairs, in this chaos of events, and with the future in darkness and, to put it briefly, given the power of Fortune—you alone of all these thousands of mortals, you want to live without care or worry? Think about what you are saying, mortal. See what you are asking. As for that complaint about not living a life of your own, for yourself, you don't mean that you have lived in poverty, but rather that you have lived in dependence. This is indeed, as you say, a most wretched state. Still, if you look around, you will see very few men actually live on their own. For even those who are thought to be the happiest and for whom others supposedly have lived their lives, these "happy" people testify through their relentless labors and anxieties that they too live their lives for others. Who? you may ask. I remind you only of the most obvious example: What of Julius Caesar? His true, albeit arrogant, motto was "The human race lives subject to the few." Yet after he had so subdued the human race so that it indeed lived by his will alone, did he not also live for others? Who? you will ask. What others? Those, clearly, who killed him: Brutus, Cimber, and the other authors of the evil conspiracy whose greedy desires even Caesar's bountiful generosity could not satisfy.[68]

Franciscus: I confess that you have brought me to my senses. I am no longer outraged at my poverty or my dependence on others.

Augustinus: You should instead by outraged that you are not wise, for wisdom alone can offer liberty and true wealth. For the rest, whoever calmly accepts the absence of causes and at the same time complains that he does not possess the effects of those causes, this person has little understanding of either cause or effect. But now describe what weighs you down, beyond the things you have already mentioned. Is it the fragility of the body? Some hidden anxiety?

Franciscus: Certainly, whenever I think about my condition, my body has seemed a burden to me. But, having seen the heavy awkward-

---

[68]Julius Caesar, the first emperor of Rome, was killed in an assassination plot that involved, among others, Brutus and Cimber. Caesar's reign signaled the end the Roman republic.

ness of the bodies of others, I must say that I have in my own body a fairly obedient possession. If only I could say the same of my soul! But it rules me.

Augustinus: May it too be brought under the rule of reason! But back to the body. What about it bothers you?

Franciscus: Nothing, except the things that vex everyone. It's mortal; it entangles me in its sufferings; it weighs me down; it urges sleep when my spirit is awake; it subjects me to other human necessities that it would be unpleasant and tedious to enumerate.

Augustinus: Calm down, please. Remember that you were born human. Before you know it, these anxieties will have ceased. If anything beyond this troubles you, tell me.

Franciscus: Perhaps the enormity of Fortune's harsh treatment of me has remained unknown to you? That in a single day, with one wicked stroke, she dashed me to pieces along with my hopes, my resources, my family, my home?

Augustinus: I see your eyes welling up, and I move on. Now is not the time to teach but rather to warn. Therefore, let it suffice that I have given this admonition: Consider the disasters that have, throughout time, befallen not only private families but also famous empires—the readings of the tragedies will have helped significantly—so that you are not ashamed that your own humble abode has been destroyed along with so many regal palaces. No go on. These few words will provide you with material for extended reflection.

Franciscus: Who could adequately describe my boredom and loathing at daily life here in the saddest, most troubled city in the whole world, this cramped, final repository of all the filth of the world?[69] Who could capture in words the nauseating spectacle that assaults from all directions—disease-ridden streets, dirty pigs running with rabid dogs, the deafening screech of wheels shaking the walls, big carriages hurtling down cross streets. And so many different kinds of people! The horrific display of beggars side by side with the mad frenzy of the wealthy, the former trapped in misery, the latter wallowing in idle pleasure and excess. And finally, such diverse people, such a variety of activity, such a confused cacophony of voices, and people running each other over in the streets. All this deranged activity wears out the senses of those accustomed to a better life and rips out the calm from generous souls and disrupts serious

---

[69]Petrarch is referring to Avignon, where the pope resided from 1309 to 1377. Petrarch argued strenuously that the pope and his curia should return to Rome.

study. And so, even as I ask God to free me from these treacherous waters with an intact ship, it seems to me, as I look around, that I have descended while alive down into the inferno. Now go, I tell myself, go do something useful, go occupy yourself with noble thoughts. "Now go, compose your melodious verses!"[70]

Augustinus: This line from Horace reveals what you most regret. You are sad because you find yourself in a place inhospitable to your studies, because, as the same poet says, "writers seek out the woods and flee cities."[71] And you expressed this same idea using other words in one of your letters: "The forests please the muses; the city is the poet's enemy."[72] If, however, the internal turmoil of your mind were quiet, this relentless din around you, though it would assail your senses, would not unsettle your soul. But lest I repeat what is already familiar to you, you have Seneca's useful letter on this subject,[73] and you have his book *On the Tranquillity of the Soul.* And for combating all sickness of the mind, you have the outstanding book by Cicero, dedicated to Brutus, which records the third day of conversations held at his villa in Tusculum.[74]

Franciscus: You know that I have read all of those works very carefully.

Augustinus: What then? You got no help from them?

Franciscus: They helped a lot while I was reading them. But as soon as the book left my hands, my connection to it likewise disappeared.

Augustinus: This is a common way of reading, and as a result of it, a hateful monstrosity has emerged: utterly disgraceful crowds of so-called men of letters. They wander here and there. They have much to say in the classroom about how to live well, but they put none of it into practice. But as for you, if you would make notes of important points, you would benefit from your reading.

Franciscus: What kind of notes?

Augustinus: Whenever you come across salutary ideas as you read, ideas that excite or captivate your soul, do not trust yourself to retain them, but work them deep into your memory and make them most familiar to you through diligent study, so that just like experienced doctors, no matter when or where some urgent illness

---

[70]Horace, *Letters* II, 2, 76.
[71]Ibid., 77.
[72]Petrarch, *Metrical Epistles* II, 3, 43.
[73]Seneca, *Moral Letters to Lucilius* 56.
[74]Franciscus is referring to the third book of Cicero's *Tusculan Disputations.*

strikes, you have the cure, as it were, written in your soul. For there are some passions of the soul, just as there are some diseases of the body, in which delay is so deadly that if you defer the remedy, hope for a cure disappears. Who does not know, for example, that certain impulses are so sudden and strong that, unless reason checks them at the outset, they destroy the soul, the body, and the whole person, no matter what remedy is later applied? Of this sort of impulse, anger is, I think, the most prominent. Not for nothing did those thinkers who divide the soul into three parts—reason in the head as a citadel, anger in the heart/breast, and desire lower still in the loins—place the locus of anger below that of reason. They did this so that reason would be ready to force back the violent impulses of the plagues beneath it and from high up call for their retreat. And because with anger this kind of restraint is more necessary, reason is placed closer to it.

Franciscus: Certainly, you are right. And to show that I have taken this truth not only from the philosophers but also from the poets, I have often thought that Virgil, when he describes the fury of the winds lying in deep caves and mountains rising above them, and King Aeolus sitting on high and restraining the winds with his power, could be describing anger and other impulses of the soul. Those passions burning deep in the breast that, unless they are restrained by the bridle of reason, as we read in the same poem, "would in their fury carry off the seas and the earth and the depths of the sky and drag them off through the air."[75] By "earth" Virgil means nothing other than the earthly material of the human body. By "seas" he means the moisture through which we live. By "depths of the sky" what else does he mean but the soul dwelling deep within and which elsewhere he says "is a fiery power whose origins are divine"?[76] It is as if he said that anger and other impulses of the soul will drive the body, the soul, indeed the whole human person over whom they rule to destruction. On the other hand, by mountains and the king sitting up on high, what could Virgil mean if not the citadel of the head and reason, which dwells there? And he says, "There, in a vast cave, King Aeolus restrains by his might the swirling winds and blustering tempests and reins them in with chains and bars. The indignant storms rage with great furor around the mountains confining them. Aeolus sits in the highest citadel

---

[75]Virgil, *Aeneid* I, 58–59.
[76]Ibid., VI, 730.

holding his scepter."[77] That is what Virgil says. As for me, as I have studied each word carefully, I have heard the fury, I have heard the gusting winds, I have heard the blustering storms, I have heard the raging and the furor. These can be understood to describe anger. And likewise, I have seen the king sitting on his high throne, I have seen him holding his scepter, I have seen him using his power to restrain, I have seen him reining in with bars and chains. Who doubts that this can designate reason? However, to establish that all this is about the soul and anger stirring up the soul, see what Virgil adds: "He soothes their souls and allays their anger."[78]

Augustinus: I approve of these meanings hidden in the poetic narrative, so many of which you, as I see, now uncover. For whether Virgil himself intended these meanings when he wrote, or whether they were the farthest thing from his mind and he meant to describe a storm and nothing more, nonetheless what you have said about anger and the power of reason, I think, has been spoken both eloquently and accurately. But to return to where I left off, always pay attention to things that can be used against anger and other impulses of the soul and especially against that plague of melancholy that has long preoccupied us. During your reading—this is what I started to say earlier—when you come upon such things, put marks next to the useful passages. Through these marks, as with hooks, you can hold in your memory useful things that wish to fly away. By this method, you will stand firm both against other things and against that sadness of the soul which, like some dark and deadly cloud, utterly destroys the seeds of virtue and all the fruits of understanding, and in which—as Cicero so eloquently put it—"lie the source and origin of all misery."[79] For certainly, if you carefully examine both yourself and others, leaving aside that there is no one without many reasons for sadness, especially leaving aside that the memory of your transgressions is, of course, a source of sadness and anxiety for you (this kind of sadness can in fact be salutary, provided, of course, that despair does not creep in), then you will confess that much has been given to you from heaven, which, among your many quarrels and complaints, can offer reason for consolation and joy.

[77]Ibid., I, 52–57.
[78]Ibid., 57.
[79]Cicero, *Tusculan Disputations* IV, 38, 83.

As for your complaint that you have not yet lived for yourself or that you are sickened by the tumult of cities, you can take comfort in the fact that greater men have voiced similar complaints and in the thought that you have fallen into this disaster by your own will and by your own will you can emerge from it, if you begin to want this wholeheartedly. Here too daily experience will help, if you have taught your ears to hear in the noise of the crowd only the delightful sound of trickling water.

But, as I said, you would accomplish this most easily if you would first restrain the commotion in your mind. For clouds and clamor surround a serene breast in vain. And so just like one sitting safe and dry on shore, you will watch the shipwrecks of others, and you will hear in silence the miserable voices of those floundering at sea. And even as you have felt compassion at this chaotic spectacle, so you will feel joy at the security of your fate compared to the dangers of others. Given these things, I am sure that you will keep away all sadness of soul.

Franciscus: Although I question much that you say, and especially your claim that to leave the city is a simple matter of will, nonetheless, because you have used reason to outdo me in many matters, I wish to lay down arms before I am completely wiped out.

Augustinus: Are you able, then, having left behind this sadness, to reconcile yourself to your fortune?

Franciscus: I am surely able, supposing that there is such a thing as fortune. For, as you know, there is such controversy about this between the Greek poet and our Latin poet that, whereas the former never deigns to use the word *fortune* in his works, as if he did not believe in it, the latter often uses the word and in some places calls fortune all-powerful.[80] This opinion is shared by a celebrated historian and an outstanding orator. For Sallust says that in all things fortune surely dominates, and Cicero did not hesitate to proclaim that fortune ruled human affairs.[81] As for what I think, perhaps I will talk about that at another time, in another place. But with regard to the task at hand, your advice has so benefitted me that when I compare my condition with that of most human beings, it does not seem as wretched as it once did.

---

[80] Petrarch is referring to Homer (the Greek poet) and Virgil (our Latin poet).
[81] See Sallust, *The Conspiracy of Catiline* 8, 1; Cicero, *For Marcellus* 2, 7.

Augustinus: I am happy if I have benefitted you in some way. I want to help you even more. But, as we have talked enough for today, would you be willing to put off the issues that remain to a third day, when we will finish our conversation?

Franciscus: Truly, I love the number three with my whole being, not so much because of the three graces as because it is held to be the number that is most akin to the divine. And this is the conviction not only of you and others who profess the true religion and who have absolute faith in the Trinity. So do the pagan philosophers, who used this number in the worship of their gods. My beloved Virgil, in fact, seems to have known this when he said, "God delights in the uneven number."[82] For the context here makes clear that he means three. Therefore, I will await from your hand the final part of your three-part gift.

THIRD DIALOGUE

Augustinus: If so far my words have brought you any help, then I beg and implore you to be open to what I still have to say. Put aside your combativeness and your contentious spirit.

Franciscus: Consider it done. For I feel that your advice has in large part freed me from my suffering, and so I come better prepared to hear what else you have to say.

Augustinus: I have not yet probed your most resistant and deeply buried wounds, and I dread doing this. I remember how much quarreling and contention resulted from even my slightest touch. I hope, however, that it will be different now. I hope that since you have collected and steeled yourself, your soul will be stronger and will bear with more equanimity my harsher criticisms.

Franciscus: Don't hesitate, please. I have grown accustomed both to hearing my diseases described and to enduring the healing hand of my physician.

Augustinus: You are still held down on either side by two adamantine, strong as steel chains. These do not allow you to think about life or death. I have always feared that these chains would destroy you. And I will not be relieved of this fear until I see that those chains have been broken and cast off and that you are unbound and perfectly free. Although it won't be easy, I believe that this could hap-

[82]Virgil, *Eclogues* 8, 75.

pen. Otherwise, I would be laboring in vain, running around in circles. Just as they say the blood of a goat works with amazing efficacy to break a diamond, so by this same method can the hardness of hearts be softened. Once the blood has touched a bitter heart, it breaks it open and penetrates it.

Nonetheless, I am afraid, because in undertaking this difficult task I need your cooperation, which you might not be able—or I should say might not be willing—to give. I am very afraid that the brilliance of these glittering hard chains, so dazzling and pleasing to your eyes, might stand in your way. Maybe you will act as I imagine a chained-up miser would act if while in jail he were bound with shackles made of gold. He might wish to be freed, but he would not wish to lose such glittering chains. In your case, the condition of your bondage is such that unless you break these chains, you cannot be free.

Franciscus: Alas, I am in even worse shape than I thought. You are saying that two chains ensnare my soul and I don't even know it?

Augustinus: And they are easy enough to see. You, however, delighted by their beauty, imagine them to be not chains but great jewels. And, to extend the analogy, you are like someone who, bound tight at the wrists and ankles with golden chains, looks with pleasure at the gold but does not see the fetters. Even now that your eyes are open, you do see what binds you but—what blindness!—you remain delighted by the very chains that drag you to your death. Worse still, you boast about them.

Franciscus: What are these chains that you are describing?

Augustinus: Love and glory.

Franciscus: The gods must deceive me! What am I hearing? You call these chains? You would—if I were to allow it—you would actually break them?

Augustinus: I do indeed set this as my task, but I am not sure what will happen. For all the other bonds that held you back were both more fragile and less pleasing to you, so that, as I broke them, you acquiesced and even approved. But though they are injurious, these two chains delight you; they deceive you with a kind of false charm, and so they require more work from me. And you will resist my efforts, as if I wanted to rob you of your greatest good. Nonetheless, I will try.

Franciscus: What have I done to deserve such things from you, that you would seek to rip out my most glorious occupations and to condemn to perpetual darkness the most serene part of my soul?

Augustinus: Oh, wretched one! Have you forgotten the philosophical saying that the ultimate depth of misery is reached when deadly persuasion has so drawn us to false opinions that we see them as the only truth?

Franciscus: That maxim has not escaped me, but it is not relevant to this discussion. Why should I not think that things in this matter must be as I see them? For certainly I have never exercised, nor will I ever exercise, better judgment than when I assert the absolute nobility of these two passions for which you reproach me.

Augustinus: Let us treat these two passions separately for now, while I search for remedies. Otherwise, I may get distracted by first one, then the other, and thus put up a weaker attack. Because we first mentioned love, we will start there. Do you not consider love the most extreme madness of all?

Franciscus: To be completely honest, I think that love can be called either the most loathsome passion or the noblest deed, depending on what is loved.[83]

Augustinus: Please, offer an example of what you mean.

Franciscus: If I desire an infamous, immoral woman, then that desire is the height of insanity. But if a rare model of virtue attracts me and if I devote myself to loving and venerating her, what do you say about that? Do you really think that there is no distinction between these two very different cases? Doesn't propriety matter at all?[84]

As for me, so that I might speak for myself, just as I judge the love in the first example a heavy and unfortunate burden, so I think that the love in the second example could not be a greater blessing. But if it seems otherwise to you, let each follow his own opinion. For there is, as you know, both a great variety of opinion and great freedom of individual judgment.

Augustinus: When evidence is contradictory, opinions are diverse. But truth is always one and the same.

Franciscus: I agree that you are right about this. But here is what leads us astray: We cling tenaciously to ancient opinions, and we do not easily turn away from them.

Augustinus: If only you understood the whole question of love as clearly as you understand that one point.

---

[83]Franciscus is making an explicit distinction between passion (*passio,* whose root meaning is "suffering," from the verb *patior*) and deed (*actio,* from *ago,* "to do").

[84]Petrarch uses the word *pudor,* translated here as "propriety." *Pudor* can mean respect, good manners, modesty, or a sense of what is appropriate, but it can also mean shame or a cause for shame.

Franciscus: What more is there? I think I understand clearly — so clearly, in fact, that I judge contrary views to be insane.

Augustinus: To accept a lie as truth just because it is old and to judge a truth to be a lie just because it is newly discovered, as if all authority were based on time, this indeed is the height of dementia.

Franciscus: You are wasting your time with this discussion. I will yield to no one on this issue of love, and that saying of Cicero comes to my aid: "If I err in this, then I err willingly, and while I live, I do not want my error taken from me."[85]

Augustinus: But Cicero used these words to put forth the very beautiful opinion that the soul is immortal. He wanted to show how he did not doubt this at all and how he did not want to hear any contrary views. You, on the other hand, abuse these same words by expressing an utterly false and abominable opinion. For surely even if the soul were mortal, still it would be better to think it was immortal, and this healthy error could even be understood to inspire a love of virtue — though this ought to be loved for its own sake even if hope of future reward is taken away. For desire for virtue would surely grow weak with the proposition of a mortal soul. On the other hand, even if it were a lie, the promise of a future life made for the purpose of inspiring the souls of mortals seems to have good effects. But you see what effects your error would have! It would hurl the soul down into madness, where fear and modesty and that which usually reins in the passions — namely, all reason and perception of truth — will perish.

Franciscus: I said already that you are wasting your time. For I remember that I have never loved anything immoral or base and indeed I have loved nothing but the most beautiful.

Augustinus: But as you know, beautiful things can be loved in a base way.

Franciscus: I have sinned neither in noun nor adverb, neither in what I loved nor in how I loved it. Do not torment me further.

Augustinus: What then? Do you wish, like certain frenzied or delirious people, to breathe your last among jokes and laughs? Or would you prefer that some remedy be applied to your still woefully sick soul?

Franciscus: Well, I won't spit out the remedy if you show me that I am sick, but for healthy people the ingestion of remedies is often deadly.

Augustinus: As is the case with many, so it is with you: Only as you convalesce will you realize how gravely ill you were.

[85]See Cicero, *On Old Age,* 23, 85.

Franciscus: I cannot in the end reject your advice, from which I myself have often benefitted greatly, especially over these past few days. Go ahead.

Augustinus: First, then, I would like you to bear with me if, compelled by our subject, I attack things in which you take pleasure. For I can now foresee how heavy the truth will sound to your ears.

Franciscus: Before you begin, answer me this: Do you know for yourself the subject about which you will speak?

Augustinus: I have considered everything carefully. Our conversation concerns a mortal woman whom, I am sad to say, you have spent a great part of your life admiring and worshiping. I am shocked at such persistent and extreme madness in a mind such as yours.[86]

Franciscus: Spare me your outrage, please. Thais and Livia were mortal women.[87] Furthermore, don't you know that you intend to discuss a woman whose mind, ignorant of earthly cares, burns only with heavenly desires; a woman whose resplendent face, if truth means anything, exhibits a kind of divine beauty; a woman whose mores exemplify probity and honesty? Neither her voice nor the force of her gaze represent anything mortal, nor is her bearing that of a human being. Consider this, I ask you, consider it again and again. I believe you will understand which words must be used in discussing her.

Augustinus: You are out of your mind. Is this how you have fed the flames of your soul for the past sixteen years, with empty flattery and soothing banalities? Even our most renowned enemy from antiquity did not occupy Italy for a longer time, nor did Italy then endure more frequent attacks or burn with more fiery flames at the hands of Hannibal than you have endured from this violent passion. In Italy, someone was finally found who compelled the greatest of enemies to go. Who will ever turn your Hannibal from your neck if you forbid him to leave and instead, of your own free will, sub-

---

[86]The woman is Laura, the inspiration for much of Petrarch's poetry.

[87]**Thais:** The name of both a historical figure, an Athenian hetaera who accompanied Alexander the Great to Asia, and a literary hetaera in *The Eunuch,* a Latin play by the Roman poet Terence (ca. 190–159 B.C.E.). In classical Greece, there were primarily three kinds of free women: wives, concubines, and hetaerae. Hetaerae, which we can translate as "companions," were high-class professional escorts. More educated than other women, they accompanied men to social functions and other public venues where wives and concubines could not go. **Livia:** A politically ambitious woman (58 B.C.E.– 29 C.E.) who was first married to Nero, with whom she had a son, the future emperor Tiberius. After a divorce, she married the emperor Augustus.

serviently extend him an invitation to stay? How you take pleasure in your own evil![88]

However, when the eyes that have fatally captivated you are closed forever; when you gaze at her body, transformed by death, and at her lifeless limbs, drained of color, you will be ashamed to have committed your immortal soul to a dead piece of flesh; and what you now so relentlessly extol will make you burn with shame.

Franciscus: God forbid that I see this premonition come to pass!

Augustinus: It will inevitably come to pass.

Franciscus: I know. But the stars are not so hostile to me that they would disturb the order of nature when it comes to her death. I was born first; I shall die first.

Augustinus: You remember, I think, a time when you feared the opposite, and, imagining that she was about to die, you wrote a funeral poem for her expressing your grief.

Franciscus: I remember that. How sad I was, and now remembering still makes me tremble. I was angry that I might be cut off from the noblest part of my soul, that I might be left to outlive the one whose simple existence made life sweet. The poem laments this feeling of loss, which came forth from me drenched with tears. I remember the sense of it, whether or not I remember the exact words.

Augustinus: I am not interested in how many tears or how much grief the fear of her death evoked in you. What concerns me is that you understand that the dread that once struck you can come back, and all the more easily, both because each day brings her closer to death and because that exceptional body, worn-out by disease and frequent childbearing, has lost much of its original strength.

Franciscus: And I also have become advanced in years and burdened with anxieties. And so I have rushed toward death with her close behind.

Augustinus: What madness it is to speculate about the order of death from the order of birth! For what do aged, bereft parents lament if not the untimely deaths of their children? What do elderly nurse-maids mourn if not the inevitable passing of their charges, "whom, deprived of sweet life and ripped from the breast, an evil day

---

[88]Hannibal (ca. 247–181 B.C.E.) was the renowned Carthaginian leader and enemy of Rome during the Second Punic War (218–201 B.C.E.). He was defeated by Scipio Africanus (ca. 236–183 B.C.E.), the hero of Petrarch's epic poem *Africa,* at a battle near Zama in 202 B.C.E.

carried off and buried with a bitter funeral?"[89] As for you, the few years by which you preceded her gives you the utterly vain hope that you will die before the fuel that feeds your passion. And you imagine this to be an unalterable law of nature.

Franciscus: Not an unalterable law of nature, as if I did not know that things could happen otherwise. But I pray diligently that they do not, and whenever I think of her death, that line from Ovid comes to my aid: "May that day be far off, and after my life has ended."[90]

Augustinus: I can't bear to listen to these inane ramblings any longer. Since you do realize that she could die before you, what will you say if she does die?

Franciscus: What else could I say? Although thrown into deep despair by that calamity, I would nonetheless take comfort from my memories of past times, times when she was alive. But may the winds snatch these words as we speak them, may storms scatter and disperse this evil prediction!

Augustinus: How can you be so blind? Do you still not understand how demented it is to have entrusted your soul to mortal things that inflame it with the heat of passion, that will never bring it rest, and that are not able to endure forever? Mortal things that torture with endless distractions the one whom they promise to soothe?

Franciscus: If you have a better argument, use it. You will never scare me with the ones you have put forth. For I did not entrust, as you think, my soul to a mortal thing. You know that I have loved not so much her body as her soul, delighted as I was by a way of life that transcends the human condition. By her example I am taught how one lives among the angels. And so if—torture to imagine!—she deserts me by dying first, you ask what I would do? I would console myself in my sadness with Laelius, wisest of Romans: "I loved the virtue of that one, which has not died."[91] I would tell myself this and other things that I hear he said after the death of the one whom he adored with such rare love.

Augustinus: You stand unmoving in an impenetrable prison of deceit, and it will take effort to force you from it. And because I see that in your condition you will more patiently listen to honest statements about yourself, rather than about her, go ahead and heap on your little woman all the praises that you want. I will not argue with you

[89] Virgil, *Aeneid* VI, 428–29.

[90] Ovid, *Metamorphoses* XV, 868.

[91] See Cicero, *On Friendship* 27, 102. Laelius is speaking of Scipio. Franciscus adapts the quotation.

about it. Call her a queen, call her a saint, call her "a goddess, a sister of Phoebe, or a child of the nymphs."[92] Not even her enormous virtue will provide you the slightest excuse for your error.

Franciscus: I wonder what new fight you are about to pick with me.

Augustinus: There can be no doubt that beautiful things can be loved in a base way.

Franciscus: I have already spoken to this point. If the love that rules me could be seen, it would resemble the face of the one whom I have praised greatly, though less than she deserves. And with Truth standing here as my witness, I declare that there has never, ever been anything base or obscene in my love, never anything culpable except for its intensity. Consider these facts together with the limit that I established, and nothing more beautiful than my love can be imagined.

Augustinus: I can respond to you in the words of Cicero: "You seek a limit for vice."[93]

Franciscus: Not vice, but love.

Augustinus: And Cicero, when he said this, was also speaking of love. Do you remember the text?

Franciscus: How could I not? I read that in the *Tusculan Disputations.* But he had in mind the love that is common among human beings. In my case, there are special qualities to it.

Augustinus: But perhaps it seems the same to each of us when we think of our own situations. For it is true with other things, but especially when it comes to love, that each person is a benevolent interpreter of his own situation. Not without cause is the following saying praised, though it was written by a common poet: "To each his own beloved, and to me mine; To each his own love, and to me mine."[94]

Franciscus: Would you like, if time allows, for me to describe a few of her many qualities that would compel you to admiration and amazement?

Augustinus: Do you think that I don't know that "those who love create their own dreams"?[95] This verse is well known in all the schools.

[92] Virgil, *Aeneid* I, 328–29.

[93] Cicero, *Tusculan Disputations* IV, 18, 41.

[94] Cicero, *Letters to Atticus* XIV, 20, 3. Cicero is quoting from the poetry of Atilius, whom he calls *"poeta durissimus,"* a most uncultivated poet. Augustinus uses the adjective *plebeius,* meaning "common" both in the sense of "not patrician" and in the sense of "vulgar."

[95] Virgil, *Eclogues* 8, 108.

Furthermore, it is shameful to hear these rantings from the mouth of someone who ought to speak and think in more elevated ways.

Franciscus: On this one point—ascribe it to gratitude or ineptitude—I will not be silent. For whatever worthiness you see in me I possess because of her, and I would never have attained whatever reputation or glory I now have if she had not nobly cultivated the fragile seed of virtue that nature placed in my breast. She called my young soul back from all turpitude. She dragged it back, as they say, with a hook and compelled it to desire higher things. How could I not be transformed in accordance with the character of such a beloved? For no slanderer can be found who is so vicious that he would turn his sharp teeth on her. None can be found who would dare to say that he has seen anything deserving reproach even in a word or a gesture of hers, let alone in her actions. The critics who leave no one unscathed pass over her in admiration and awe. And so it is not at all astonishing that this name, which is so honored, has inspired in me the desire for a more brilliant reputation and has eased the hard labors through which I pursue higher things. For what else was I desiring as a young man than that I please her, and her alone, she who alone had been so pleasing to me?

And so that I might succeed in this, I have spurned a thousand seductive pleasures, and you know how many cares and labors I have imposed upon myself even as a man in his prime. And still you demand that I forget her or love her less, this woman who took me away from the common concerns of the crowd and who, as my leader in all things, goaded my sluggish mind and aroused my half-sleeping soul?

Augustinus: You are indeed a wretched man! How much better it would have been for you to stay silent rather than to speak! For although even in silence I would have seen how you are on the inside, nonetheless this vehement and relentless defense of yours has moved me to anger and nausea.

Franciscus: Why, I ask you?

Augustinus: Because to think what is false is only a sign of ignorance. But to impudently defend what is false is a sign of both ignorance and pride.

Franciscus: What is it that so clearly demonstrates that I have argued falsely?

Augustinus: Only every word that you say, above all when you say that you are who you are because of her. If you think she gave you this life, then you are clearly wrong. But if you think that she has kept you from achieving more, then you speak the truth. How great a man you could have been if she had not dragged you back with the allure of beauty. What you are, therefore, the goodness of nature gave you. What you could have been, that she snatched away, or rather you threw it away. She is innocent. Her beauty seemed to you so enticing, so sweet, that it ravaged with the flames of burning desire and torrential storms of tears all crops able to grow from your native seeds of virtue.

Furthermore, you boast falsely that she dragged you back from all turpitude. Perhaps she dragged you back from many perils, but she pushed you into still more. Neither he who, in showing you how to avoid a sordid path, leads you off a precipice nor he who, while curing your small wounds, inflicts a fatal blow to the jugular deserves to be called a liberator rather than a killer. So it is with this woman. She whom you vaunt as your leader has, while dragging you away from many lewd things, pushed you into a splendid abyss. And to go on, this claim that she taught you to focus on higher things and that she took you away from the common lot of humans really means only that you sat at her feet, captivated by her sweetness alone, assiduously neglecting and utterly contemptuous of everything else. When it comes to human affairs, you know that there is nothing more troublesome than that.

Now when you say that she has entangled you in innumerable arduous tasks, on this topic alone you speak the truth. Consider, however, why you find this to be such a great gift. Certainly, there are many different tasks that it would be wrong to avoid. But what dementia it is to seek out new such labors of your own free will! When you boast that through her you are eager for a more brilliant reputation, here I have compassion for your error. Certainly, of the burdens borne by your soul, I will show that there is none more destructive than this. But our conversation is not yet at that point.

Franciscus: The ever alert fighter threatens and then strikes. Furthermore, I am shaken both by the threat and the blow, and now I begin to lurch wildly.

Augustinus: How much more wildly you will stumble when I inflict the most serious wound! For there is no doubt that this woman whom you celebrate, this woman to whom you claim to owe everything, actually destroys you.

Franciscus: Good God, how will you ever persuade me of this?

Augustinus: She has kept your soul aloof from the love of heavenly things, and she has turned your desire from the Creator toward a mere creature. And this is the one sure way leading down to death.

Franciscus: Do not, I ask you, pass judgment hastily. It is certain that love for her is responsible for my love for God.

Augustinus: But that perverts the order of things.

Franciscus: How?

Augustinus: Because although each creature ought to be loved out of love for the Creator, you, captivated by the seductions of a creature, have in your perversity not loved the Creator as he ought to be loved. Instead, you have wondered at his skill, as if, out of all of his works, he had created nothing more lovely than this woman, when in fact the least significant kind of beauty is that belonging to the physical body.

Franciscus: Truth is my witness and my conscience corroborates that (as I have already said before) I have not loved her body more than her soul. This is something that you can see for yourself, because the more she advances in age, that great destroyer of physical beauty, the more adamantly I persist in my devotion. For, although the flower of youth clearly wilts with the passage of time, years enhance the grace of the soul, which, just as it nourished my love at the beginning, so now it sees to the perpetuation of what it began. Otherwise, if I had been driven by the beauty of her body, my intentions would have changed long ago.

Augustinus: Are you kidding me? You think that the same soul in a squalid and misshapen body would have similarly pleased you?

Franciscus: Certainly, I do not dare to say that. For the soul cannot be seen, and that kind of body would not have attested that such a soul lay within. But if it were visible to the eyes, I would certainly love the beauty of the soul in spite of its deformed dwelling place.

Augustinus: You are using verbiage as a crutch. For if you can only love what you can see with your eyes, then you loved her body. Nonetheless, I do not deny that her soul and her way of life offered nourishment to your desires. Indeed, this is indisputable since (as I will argue a little later) her very name contributed not a little but a lot to your madness. For in all passions of the soul, but especially in this one, great conflagrations rise from the smallest of embers.

Franciscus: I see where you are pushing me. You clearly want me to admit, with Ovid, that "I loved her soul with her body."[96]

---

[96] Ovid, *The Loves* I, 10, 13.

Augustinus: You should admit this and also what follows: that you loved neither the one nor the other with appropriate moderation.

Franciscus: You will have to torture me before I will admit that.

Augustinus: There's more: that because of this love, you have fallen into great misery.

Franciscus: This I will not admit even if you put me on the rack.

Augustinus: Soon you will indeed admit to both of these things, and of your own free will, unless you ignore my arguments and questions. So tell me: Do you remember your childhood? Or perhaps all memory of previous times has vanished amidst the turmoil of your current anxieties?

Franciscus: I assure you that I remember my infancy and childhood as if they were yesterday.

Augustinus: Do you remember how much you then feared God? How often you meditated on death? How powerfully you were moved by religion? How much you loved what was upright and honest?

Franciscus: Of course I remember, and I grieve that as time progressed, my virtue declined.

Augustinus: For my part, I always feared lest a spring breeze scatter that bloom, which was growing out of season. Had it remained whole and unharmed, it would have, in its own time, produced wonderful fruit.

Franciscus: Keep to the subject. How does this pertain to the issues with which we began this discussion?

Augustinus: I'll tell you. Think silently to yourself (since you feel that you remember both the recent and the distant past), think about the whole course of your life, and remember at what point such a change in your habits appeared.

Franciscus: There, in the blink of an eye, I have reviewed the course of my years.

Augustinus: And what do you find?

Franciscus: That the story of the Pythagorean Y, which I have heard and read, is not stupid.[97] For, as I was ascending by the virtuous path, still moderate and sober, I came to a crossroads. I was ordered to take up the path on the right. Instead, I can't say whether out of recklessness or obstinacy, I turned down to the left. Nor was what I

---

[97] See Lactantius, *Divine Institutes* VI, 3. Lactantius writes that human life is like the letter *Y* because each person comes to a place where he or she makes a crucial choice. In his explanation, Lactantius quotes a line from the *Aeneid* that Petrarch also quotes here.

had often read as a boy of help to me: "Here is a place where the road divides into two parts: The one on the right, which leads past the threshold of the great god Dis, is our way to Elysium; but the path on the left inflicts punishments on the evil and sends us to impious Tartarus."[98] Although I had read these things before, I did not understand them until I had experienced them. And so I was distracted by the circuitous and sordid path, and, though often turning to look back in tears, I could not stay on the right-hand path. At that time, from the moment I deserted it, the turmoil in my way of life began.

Augustinus: But during what period of your life did this happen?

Franciscus: During the fever of adolescence. If you wait a minute, I will easily recall how old I was when it happened.

Augustinus: I am not asking for your exact age. Instead, tell me this: When did you first see the face of this woman of yours?

Franciscus: That I will never forget.

Augustinus: Put this date together with the date at which your way of life degenerated.

Franciscus: My first encounter with her and my transgression did in fact occur at the same time.

Augustinus: That is all I needed to know. I think, when you met her, you were stupefied, and her rare brilliance made you shut your eyes. For they say that shock is the beginning of love. This is how the poet, who understood the order of nature, put it: "At first sight, Sidonian Dido was stupefied."[99] And this line follows later: "In love, Dido is on fire."[100] And even though, as you well know, the whole story is complete fiction, nonetheless the poet kept in mind the nature of things as he wrote. But if you were stupefied by your encounter with that woman, why specifically did you turn down the left path?

Franciscus: I think because it seemed wider and downhill. The right path is hard and narrow.

Augustinus: So you were afraid of hard work. But that much celebrated woman of yours, whom you imagine to be your surest guide

---

[98] Virgil, *Aeneid,* VI, 540–43. Petrarch's quotation is not exact. **Dis:** The god of the underworld, also called Pluto or Hades. **Elysium:** The part of the underworld where good souls go after death. **Tartarus:** The part of the underworld where bad souls go after death.

[99] Ibid., I, 613. **Dido:** The queen of Carthage. After Aeneas landed there, the goddess Venus caused her to fall in love with Aeneas. Sidonian means Phoenician and refers to Dido's origins.

[100] Ibid., IV, 101.

to the heavens, why didn't she set you straight as you stood there, anxious and hesitating? Why didn't she, as is customarily done for the blind, take your hand and advise you where you should go?

Franciscus: She did what she could. What else could she do? Moved by no entreaties, conquered by no flattery, in spite of her youth and mine, she held fast to her womanly modesty and stood unmovable and firm against many kinds of things that by rights should have moved even an adamantine spirit. Without doubt her female spirit proclaimed what was fitting for a man, and she saw to it that in pursuing a zeal for modesty, I lacked, in Seneca's words, neither an example nor a reproach. Finally, when she saw me headstrong with runaway passion, she preferred to desert rather than to follow.

Augustinus: So, at that time, you did indeed desire something base—a fact that you earlier denied. But this madness you experienced is common among lovers *[amantes]*—or, as I should say, among the demented *[amentes]*—so that a just characterization of all of you is "I want it, I don't want it, I don't want it, I want it." In fact, you have no idea what you want or don't want.

Franciscus: In my carelessness, I fell into a trap. Still, if once I did want to do something else, it was because love and youth compelled it. Now I know what I want and what I desire, and at last I have fortified my unsteady soul. She, on the other hand, resolved and single-minded from the beginning, has always stood fast. The more I understand her female constancy, the more I admire it. So, if at one time I grieved at her good judgment, now I rejoice and give thanks for it.

Augustinus: Once someone has lied to you, it is not easy to trust that person again. You will have to change your habits and your way of life before you persuade me that your soul has changed. Perhaps your desire has been softened and calmed, but the flames are certainly not extinguished. And indeed, you who attribute so much to your beloved, do you not realize how much you condemn yourself by absolving her? It pleases you to acknowledge that she is the holiest of women, while you acknowledge yourself to be demented and wicked. She is most happy, yet your love for her makes you miserable. And, if you remember, this is the point with which I began.

Franciscus: I do remember, and I am not able to deny that it is so, and I understand the position to which you have gradually led me.

Augustinus: So that you can understand more fully, listen to me. There is nothing that so produces indifference and contempt for God as love of temporal things. And especially this thing that people call by the name "Love" or even (the greatest sacrilege) call God, so that heavenly sanction assents to human madness, and a great crime becomes somehow permitted because it is imagined to be divinely inspired. Nor should it be surprising that such a feeling should dwell in human hearts. With all other objects, either the visible appearance of a thing, or the anticipated pleasure of enjoying it, or a particular impulse of our minds captivates us. But with human love, all these things together set us aflame with mutual affection. If all hope for such reciprocity is lost, love itself necessarily subsides. And so, although with other objects you only love, in this case of human love you are also loved in return, and the mortal heart is driven first by one feeling [a desire to love], then the other [a desire to be loved]. Thus it seems that our Cicero did not speak unreasonably when he said, "Out of all the passions certainly none is stronger than love."[101] This Cicero who in four books had already defended the Academy, a school of philosophy that doubts everything, must have been very convinced when he added that word *certainly*.

Franciscus: I have often noted that passage, and I have been amazed that he called love the strongest of all passions.

Augustinus: You should hardly be amazed, unless forgetfulness has taken over your soul. Nonetheless, you must be made to remember with a brief description of love's many evils. Recall now at what time that plague infected your mind. Remember how quickly you were completely turned upside down, how you became so miserable that with a kind of self-destructive pleasure, you fed on tears and sighs. Remember the sleepless nights, the name of your beloved perpetually on your lips. Remember your contempt for all things, your hatred for life, and your desire for death. Remember your sadness, your love of solitude, your flight from the company of others. Indeed, what Homer said of Bellerophon could equally be applied to you: "This man, suffering and in mourning, who wandered into foreign camps, eating his heart out, shunning all traces of humankind."[102] From this comes your pallor and your thinness; from this the flower of youth has wilted before its time. Then came the ever sad eyes that were always weeping, then a confused mind,

---

[101] Cicero, *Tusculan Disputations* IV, 35, 75.

[102] Homer, *Iliad* VI, 201–2. Petrarch is quoting from Cicero, *Tusculan Disputations* III, 26, 63. Homer recounts how Bellerophon, after a lifetime filled with tragedy and Herculean challenges, eventually incurred the wrath of the gods and was left to wander, grief-stricken and alone.

then the fitful sleep, and tearful laments in your sleep if you did manage to sleep. Your voice grew weak and hoarse from crying, the sound of your words was broken and halting, and whatever else that is imaginable, no matter how disturbing and miserable, happened to you.

Do these seem to you to be signs of health? What of the fact that each day, she was the beginning and the end of your happiness and your misery? With her coming the sun rose; her departure brought the return of night. A change in her expression changed your soul. Depending on her least gesture, you were made happy or sad. Ultimately, your existence depended entirely on her will. I am, as you know, now describing things that are true and known to everyone.

Furthermore, what could be more insane than this: Not content with the sight of her, this woman from whom all these miseries had come, you sought out another face, one made by the genius of a famous artist, so that, carrying it with you everywhere, you would always have cause for never-ending tears? Fearing, perhaps, that they might dry up, you reflected relentlessly on the one who provoked them, irresponsibly oblivious to everything else. But now I come to the supreme height of your delirium, and I will now expose what earlier I threatened. For who can adequately condemn, who can express sufficient outrage at the insanity of your alienated mind, when, captivated by the splendor not only of her body but even of her name, you sought out, to no meaningful end, whatever sounded like it? This is why you so cherished the laurel, whether imperial or poetic, because she is called by the name Laura. And since that time, you have produced scarcely a single poem that does not mention this laurel, as if you had become none other than an inhabitant of the river Peneus or a priest on Cirrha's mountain.[103] And finally, because it was wrong to hope for the imperial crown, you desired the poetic laurel, promised to you by the quality of your studies, no less modestly than you loved that woman herself. And although in order to reach your reward you were carried on the wings of genius, nonetheless you tremble now remembering for yourself with what great effort you finally achieved it.

[103]Augustinus is referring to the story of Apollo and Daphne from ancient mythology. Apollo, a god to whom Mount Parnassus (near the city of Cirrha in Thessaly) was sacred, fell in love with Daphne, the daughter of the river god Peneus. Daphne wished to remain a virgin. As Apollo chased her, she begged her father for help. He turned her into a laurel tree just as Apollo was reaching out to capture her. Augustinus likens Franciscus's devotion to the laurel to that of Peneus and Apollo.

For I am not blind to what you are thinking. I see that you have come up with a pat response and are about to deliver it. You think, in fact, that you dedicated yourself to these studies some time before you desired her, and you think that the poetic laurel had moved your soul from childhood. I am not ignorant of this, and I do not dispute it. But surely the fact that this custom had been abandoned for many centuries; the fact that contemporary times are hostile to such literary studies; and the hazards of long journeys, through which you came to the threshold not only of imprisonment but also of death and other, even more violent obstacles thrown up by Fortune, surely all of this might have compromised or frustrated your plan. Instead, the memory of her sweet name, which was perpetually goading your spirit, drove you, all other weighty cares forced aside, by land and sea among the rocks of many difficulties to Rome and Naples, where finally you achieved what you had been so fervently desiring. And if anyone finds these signs of only average folly, I would think that person himself greatly afflicted. I knowingly leave out that passage from Terence's play *The Eunuch,* which Cicero was not ashamed to borrow: "In love are all these evils: injuries, suspicions, quarrels, truces, war then peace again."[104] Doubtless you recognize your own insanity in his words, especially your jealousy. For just as love is the most powerful of all the passions, so jealousy is the dominant aspect of the plague of love.

But perhaps you will reply, saying, "I do not deny these things, but reason exists, and by its will these passions are tempered." Terence expected that you would respond in this way when he added, "If you expect through reason to make certain things out of these uncertain struggles, you do nothing but seek to lose your mind in a reasonable way."[105]

With this said, and you no doubt recognize it as true, all of your escape routes are, unless I am mistaken, blocked. These miseries and others like them are the accoutrements of love. The precise enumeration of them is neither necessary for those who have experienced them nor credible to those who have not. Nonetheless, the greatest danger of all (to return to our topic) is that it causes equally forgetfulness of God and forgetfulness of self. For how can a soul, bowed down with the weight of such evils and able only to crawl on the ground, hope to arrive at the one and purest font of

[104]Terence, *The Eunuch* I, 1, 59–61, quoted in Cicero, *Tusculan Disputations* IV, 35, 76.
[105]Terence, ibid., 1, 61–63.

the true good? And since this is how things are, you should no longer be astonished that to Cicero, no passion of the soul seemed more violent than love.

Franciscus: I have been conquered, I confess, because you seem to have taken all the things you describe directly from the book of my own experiences. And so allow me, since you have mentioned Terence's *Eunuch,* to add a complaint taken from the same place: "Oh, unworthy crime! Now I feel miserable and disgusted. I burn with love, and though I am prudent, knowing, aware, and seeing my plight, I die, and I do not know what I can do."[106] Now allow me to demand advice from you using the words of the same poet: "Therefore, while there is time, think and think again."[107]

Augustinus: I too will give my response in the words of Terence: "You cannot use a plan to guide a thing that has neither plan nor rationale."[108]

Franciscus: What, then, am I supposed to do? Should I surrender to despair?

Augustinus: First, we must try all remedies. Now accept without delay this time-tested advice: On this topic of love, you know that there have been written not only remarkable treatises by outstanding philosophers but also whole books by illustrious poets. It would be insulting, especially to you, who proclaim yourself a master of these things, for me to repeat either under what circumstances these books are to be sought out or how they should be understood. But perhaps you would not consider it unfriendly for me to advise you how these things that you have read and understood can be directed toward your salvation.

First, then, as Cicero says, "Some think that an old love can be driven out by a new love as one nail is driven out by another."[109] Ovid, master of love, agrees with this advice, offering the general rule "All love is conquered by a new successor."[110] And without doubt this is true. A fragmented soul that is distracted by many objects is directed less energetically toward each one. Hence the Ganges, as they say, was divided by the king of the Persians into innumerable channels, and out of one river that had inspired fear were carved several little streams worthy only of scorn. Similarly, a

---

[106]Terence, ibid., 1, 70–73.
[107]Ibid., 56.
[108]Ibid., 57–58.
[109]Cicero, *Tusculan Disputations* IV, 35, 75. Cicero cites a Greek proverb.
[110]Ovid, *Remedies for Love* 462.

dispersed line of troops is vulnerable to the enemy, and a diffuse fire weakens. In short, as each force grows when united, so it diminishes when dispersed.

However, you must understand the implications of this remedy as I see them. For certainly we must fear that while you are being pulled away from one rather noble (if I may use this term in this context) passion, you will lose yourself in many more, and that, no longer a lover, you will become an inconstant, roaming pursuer of women. Now in my judgment, if you must inevitably die, it is some comfort to have died of a nobler disease.

So what, then, you ask, is my ultimate advice? Gather your spirit and flee from your love if you can. I do not disapprove of moving from one prison to another. For perhaps there is hope of liberty or at least of a lighter ruling power. But I do not want to see your neck, freed from one collar, carry around instead innumerable shackles of sordid servitude.

Franciscus: At this concluding point in the doctor's speech, would you permit the patient, who is aware of his disease, to say something?

Augustinus: Why would I not permit it? For many have approached the search for a fitting cure by way of the opinions of the patient, as if these were a kind of symptom.

Franciscus: Know, then, this one thing: I cannot love another. My soul is accustomed to admiring her. My eyes are used to looking at her, and whatever she is not, they interpret as obscure and ugly. And so if you command me to love another so that I can be free from this love, then you throw up before me an insurmountable obstacle. It is done; I am doomed.

Augustinus: Your sense is dulled, and your desire has been numbed. And so because you are not strong enough to take in a cure, we must use exterior remedies. Do you not think that you could persuade your soul into flight or exile, to live without the constant sight of familiar places?

Franciscus: Although I am dragged back by the most tenacious of hooks, I can do it.

Augustinus: If you can do it, you will be saved. What need I say, except to quote, with a few small changes, the line from Virgil: "Alas, flee the cherished land, flee the beloved shore."[111] For how can you ever be safe in this place, where so many traces of your wounds abound, where you are worn down both by the sight of things

---

[111]Virgil, *Aeneid* III, 44. Virgil's line is "cruel land, greedy shore."

around you and by memories of the past? This is why Cicero expresses the same thought as Virgil: "Just like a sick person who is not getting better, you will be cured by a change of scene."[112]

Franciscus: But think about what you are asking of me! How many times have I, eager to get well and not unaware of this advice, how many times have I tried and tried to flee. And although I have feigned various reasons, the one single goal of all my travels and my living in the country has always been freedom. In pursuit of freedom, I have been driven to destinations far and wide, to the west and north, even all the way to the ocean. And you see how much I have gained from this! Thus Virgil's comparison has often come to mind: "Like an unguarded doe in the groves of Crete, hit by an arrow launched by a shepherd as he hunts. Unaware of the path of the arrow, he leaves. But she wanders, fleeing, through Cretan woods and pastures, the lethal arrow clings to her side."[113] I have become like this deer. I have fled, but I carry my evil with me wherever I go.

Augustinus: What do you expect me to say now? You have answered your own question.

Franciscus: I have? How?

Augustinus: Because for someone who carries around his evil, a change of scene increases hardship but does not bring health. Therefore, what Socrates said to a certain young man who complained that his travels had done him no good, can be, not inappropriately, said to you. Socrates said, "You took yourself with you wherever you went."[114] In your case, certainly, before all else your old burdensome cares must be surrendered, and your soul must be prepared. Then you must take flight. For what is true for the body is also true for the soul: Unless the patient is well-disposed, the power of the physician is ineffective. Otherwise, you could travel to the far corners of India, and still you would find true what Horace said: "Those who travel across the sea change the view, not their souls."[115]

Franciscus: Now I am really confused. You offer me the prescription of flight for a recuperating and healing soul, yet you simultaneously proclaim that my soul must be cured and healthy before it can flee.

---

[112] Cicero, *Tusculan Disputations* IV, 35, 74. Petrarch's quotation is not exact.
[113] Virgil, *Aeneid* IV, 69–73.
[114] See Seneca, *Moral Letters to Lucilius* 104, 7.
[115] Horace, *Letters* I, 11, 27.

But this does not resolve the problem of how one gets cured. For if a person is already cured, what more is sought? And if not cured, and if a change of scene (which you yourself suggest) will not help, then tell me more explicitly what remedies should be used.

Augustinus: I did not say that the soul has to be already cured and healthy. I said that the soul must be prepared. Furthermore, either it is cured and a change of scene will sustain its health, or it is not yet cured but still prepared, and the same strategy will bring about the cure. But if neither, what would such a change of scene or constant moving from place to place accomplish, except to aggravate your sadness? I won't hesitate here to use the testimony of Horace: "I think," he said, "that reason and prudence carry away our anxieties, not the expanse of the broad, wide sea."[116] And truly, this is right. For you will go full of hope, desiring to return, dragging with you all the chains that bind your soul. Wherever you go, in whatever direction you turn, you will be thinking about the face and the words of the woman you left behind, and, as is the dubious privilege of lovers, you will see and hear her in spite of the great distance between you. You think that you can extinguish love through such tricks? Believe me, love will only burn brighter in both of you. For this reason, the authorities on love advise, among other things, that brief periods of separation be observed lest lovers grow contemptuous or bored from constantly being together. Therefore, this is my advice, my plea, my command: to teach the soul to lay down what burdens it, you must go away without hope of returning. Then you will understand what absence can contribute to the health of a soul. After all, if you chanced upon a place that was injurious and pestilential to your body, a place where you would lead a life perpetually disturbed by disease, wouldn't you flee, never to return? But perhaps, as I deeply fear, it is more important to humans to care for the body than the soul.

Franciscus: This last remark has to do with humankind as a whole. About the former, certainly there is no doubt that if I were to become sick because of an unhealthy locale, I would expel the sickness by moving to a healthier climate. And I would desire the same thing even more eagerly if it were a sickness of the soul. But this, as I see, is a more difficult kind of cure.

Augustinus: But the authority of the greatest philosophers agrees that this is in fact not true, because clearly all kinds of sicknesses of the

[116]Ibid., 25–26.

soul can be cured, except when the sick person resists it. However, there are many diseases of the body that no art can cure. For the rest, lest I am diverted too far from where I started, I maintain my original view: As I said, the soul must be prepared and instructed to abandon what it loves. It must be taught not to turn around and not to look back at the familiar things it has left behind. Only then is the journey of the lover safe. As for you, if you want your soul to be healthy, you know what must be done.

Franciscus: Let me restate it so that you see that I have understood what you have said: Journeys confer no benefit on an unprepared soul, but they make a prepared soul healthy, and they protect the state of a soul already in a state of health. Is this the aim of your three precepts?

Augustinus: That is right, and you have summarized well what was said at length.

Franciscus: Still, if no one had shown me that the first two of these were true, I could have determined it on my own. But the third proposition—that it is necessary for a soul now healthy and already led into safety to flee—this I do not understand, unless perhaps you were persuaded to say this by a fear that it might fall back.

Augustinus: Does falling back seem like a small danger to you? If such relapses are to be feared when it comes to the body, how much more should we fear them when it comes to the soul! For it is much easier and much more dangerous for a soul to go back. For this reason, Seneca said nothing more salubrious (within the realm of nature) than what he said in a certain letter: "For the one who is trying to put off love, every reminder of bodily pleasure must be forbidden, for nothing breaks out again more easily than love."[117] How true these words are, words ripped out of the innermost depths of experience. With regard to this, I need cite no witness other than yourself.

Franciscus: I confess that this is true. But when you consider it, these words are said not of one who *has already* put off love, but of one who *is trying* to put off love.

Augustinus: Seneca said it of the one for whom danger was most immediate. Any injury is more dangerous to a wound before it has scarred over, or to a sick person before he has recovered his health. However, although it is more dangerous before, such injury

---

[117]Seneca, *Moral Letters to Lucilius,* 69, 3.

is still not to be taken lightly after one has recovered. And since familiar examples penetrate more deeply into the soul, I will cite your own experience. In this very city—which, though not the cause of all your troubles, is certainly their workshop—when you thought you had recovered, so that, had you fled the city, you would have recovered, how often did you find yourself reminded of old vanities? How often, while walking through familiar neighborhoods, remembering past errors, have you, though encountering no one, been stupefied by the sight of places alone? How often have you breathed heavy sighs, stopped dead still, and finally been scarcely able to hold back the tears? And soon afterward, wounded and fleeing, you said to yourself, "I recognize that in these places there lurk tricks of some kind, tricks of an old enemy. Traces of death live here." And so, if you want my opinion, even if you were healthy, and you are certainly far from it, it would not be advisable to linger in these places. Furthermore, it is not right for someone who has been freed from his chains to wander around the walls of his former prison—a prison whose master walks around tirelessly, setting traps here, there, and especially near the feet of those whom he complains have escaped, a prison whose door is always open. "The descent to Avernus is easy; night and day, the door of black Dis is open."[118] And if the healthy must guard against these things, how much more careful must be those whom sickness has not yet deserted! Such people, those who seek but do not yet possess health, are the ones that Seneca had in mind when he offered his advice. For it would be a waste of time to counsel those who are burning with passion and do not think about their health. Seneca reached out to those at the next stage, those who still burn but who are considering leaving the flames.

The smallest drink of water has been known to injure many convalescents who would have benefitted from it before they got sick. Often a slight push will move a person when tired but will have no effect when that same person is rested and strong. How slight are the things that sometimes push a healing soul back into the greatest miseries! A glimpse of luxurious purple cloth on the back of another renews ambition. Seeing a small pile of coins invigorates avarice. The sight of a beautiful body inflames wantonness. Fluttering eyelashes excite sleeping love. These plagues come so easily

[118]Virgil, *Aeneid* VI, 126–27.

into your soul because of your dementia, and once they have learned the way in, they return all the more effortlessly.

Because this is the way it is, you must not only leave this pestilent place; you must also flee with the utmost care from what turns your soul back to its former cares, lest, in returning and looking back, you, like Orpheus, lose the Eurydice you have recovered.[119] This is the crux of my advice.

Franciscus: I embrace your advice and thank you for it. I see that there is a remedy suited to my weakness. At this point, I am considering flight, but I do not know which is the best road to take.

Augustinus: Many paths lie open to you in many different directions, many harbors along your route. I know that Italy above all pleases you and that your native soil is naturally precious to you, and not without reason: "For neither the forest of the Medes, richest of lands, nor the beautiful Ganges, nor the Hermus, swirling with gold, can contend with Italy, nor can Battra nor India nor the whole Panchaia rich with fragrant sands."[120] Indeed, in a poem written to a friend, you yourself recently expanded on this subject that our outstanding poet Virgil had so truthfully and eloquently addressed in these lines.

Therefore, I suggest you go to Italy because—given the customs of its inhabitants and its sky; given the expanse of the surrounding sea, the hills of the Apennines that divide its shores; given every aspect of its landscape—no place could be more suited to your problems. I would prefer too that you not limit yourself to one small region of Italy. Instead, go happily wherever your soul takes you. Go confidently. Hurry and don't look back. Forget the past; embrace the future. For far too long, you have been in exile, both from your country and from yourself. It's time to go back, "for the sun is setting and night is a friend to robbers."[121] I warn you using your own words.

---

[119]**Orpheus, Eurydice:** In Greek mythology, Orpheus, who was given a lyre by Apollo, produced songs of such power that animals, trees, and rocks followed the sound. When his wife, Eurydice, died, he followed her into the underworld, where his music won him back his wife, on the condition that he not look back at her until they had returned to the region above. At the last instant, he looked back to make sure that Eurydice was following him, only to see her swallowed up again.

[120]Virgil, *Georgics* II, 136–39. For the word I have translated as "fragrant," Petrarch has *turicremis* (incense-burning) and Virgil has *turiferis* (incense-bearing). **Medes:** East of the river Tigris, in present-day Iran. **Ganges:** A river in northern India. **Hermus:** A river in Aeolis, in Asia Minor. **Battra:** Bactra; a city in Persia, on the river Bactrus, along the Siberian gold route. **Panchaia:** An imaginary island east of Arabia, reputed to be full of precious stones and incense.

[121]Petrarch, *Penitential Psalms* 3, 10.

One thing remains that I almost forgot to mention. Know that you must avoid solitude for a long time, until you feel that no vestiges of your sickness remain. You should actually not have been surprised when you remembered that isolation in the country had not benefitted you at all. For what remedy, I ask you, did you expect to find in the lonely and remote countryside? I confess that, as you were fleeing there—alone, sighing, and longingly looking back at the city— I laughed from up above. I said to myself, "Look how love has brought a Lethean fog to this miserable creature and has taken away his memory of that verse that is so well known even among schoolchildren: 'Fleeing sickness, he runs to his death.'"[122]

Franciscus: You are right. But who wrote that verse?

Augustinus: Ovid: "You who love, solitary places injure you; beware of solitary places. To where do you flee? You can be safer in a crowd."[123]

Franciscus: I remember that well! I have known those lines practically since I was an infant.

Augustinus: What good is it to know a lot if you do not know how to use this knowledge to address your needs? I am all the more astonished at your error in seeking solitude, since you were aware of the contrary views of ancient authorities and you yourself have added new arguments against it. Indeed, you have often complained that you gained nothing from solitude. You have voiced this complaint in many of your writings, but especially in the poem in which you brilliantly describe your condition.[124] While you were composing it, I delighted in its sweetness, and I was stunned that such a sweet poem could come from the mouth of a crazy man struggling with such inner turmoil. What love must have moved the Muses to remain at home with you and not flee, pushed away by the inner commotion and self-hate of their host. For when Plato says, "A sane person knocks in vain at the door of poetry," and when his successor Aristotle says, "There is no great intellect without a component of madness," they have something else in mind.[125] Their words have nothing to do with your insanity. But more on this another time.

Franciscus: I confess that it is so. However, I did not think that I wrote

---

[122]**Lethean fog:** A reference to the river Lethe in the underworld, whose waters produced forgetfulness in those who drank it.

[123]Ovid, *Remedies for Love* 579–80.

[124]Petrarch, *Metrical Epistles* I, 14.

[125]Plato, *Phaedrus* 245a; Aristotle, *Poetics* 1455a, 32.

anything sweet or indeed anything that would be especially pleasing to you. Now I begin to love that poem of mine. Now if you have any other remedies, please, I implore you, do not keep them from a man in need.

Augustinus: To explain everything you know is to show off rather than to advise a friend. After all, the many kinds of remedies for internal and external diseases were not discovered so that one person could try them all. As Seneca says, "Nothing so impedes health as a rapid change in medicine, nor do healing scabs form on a wound to which many remedies are applied."[126] Rather, as one remedy fails, try another. And so, although there are a lot of remedies for your disease, I will be content to use a few, those that, out of them all, will in my view be the most effective for you. I do not seek to teach you something new in this but rather to show you what, out of things already widely known, I think would be most efficacious.

As Cicero says, there are three things that frighten the soul away from love: satiety, shame, and reflection.[127] There may be more, there may be fewer, but in order not to deviate from such an authority, let's agree that there are these three. It is pointless to discuss the first (satiety), because you will think it impossible, with things as they are, that you could ever get enough of this love.

If only your appetite would trust in reason and use past experience to consider the future, you would easily agree that however delightful something may be, not only satiety but even boredom and nausea can slowly overtake you. However, my personal experience with you tells me that I try this argument in vain, that even though you concede that satiety is possible and that when it happens it kills love, nonetheless you contend that this feeling of "enough" is the farthest possible from your burning desire, and in fact I agree. Therefore, let's turn to the two remaining remedies. You will not, I trust, deny this: that nature gave you some intelligence and a soul capable of modesty.

Franciscus: Unless I misjudge my own situation, what you say is very true, so true that often I must painfully acknowledge how ill-suited I am both to my sex and to these times when, as you see, all things go to the shameless *[impudens]*. To them fall honors, hope, and riches, and even virtue and fortune.

Augustinus: Do you not then see how great the conflict is between

---

[126]Seneca, *Moral Letters to Lucilius* 2, 3.
[127]Cicero, *Tusculan Disputations* IV, 35, 76.

these two tendencies, love and modesty *[amor et pudor]*? While love urges on the soul, modesty holds it in check. Love kicks with the spur, modesty pulls back on the reins. Love attends to nothing, modesty considers everything.

Franciscus: I see this only too well, and it pains me to be pulled in different directions by such conflicting feelings. Indeed, these feelings strike me in turn, so that I am tossed first this way, then that, as if there were a hurricane inside my head. I am as yet unsure which feeling I should wholeheartedly follow.

Augustinus: Forgive the question, but tell me: Have you looked at yourself in the mirror lately?

Franciscus: Why do you want to know that? Nothing out of the ordinary.

Augustinus: Not, I hope, more often nor with more care than is necessary. Let me ask you another question: Haven't you noticed that your face changes from day to day and that, as time passes, gray gleams on your temples?

Franciscus: And here I thought you were going to say something extraordinary. These things that you mention happen to everyone who is born: We grow up, we age, we die. I recognize in myself changes that occur in practically everyone my age. I don't know why, but people seem to age more quickly than they used to.

Augustinus: The old age of others will not bring you youth, nor will the death of others grant you immortality. Forget about everyone else and let's get back to you. So? Didn't the visible change in your appearance change your soul at all?

Franciscus: It shook my soul but did not change it.

Augustinus: At that time, how did your soul seem to you? What did you say?

Franciscus: As you can imagine, I of course thought of the words of the emperor Domitian: "As a young man I endure with equanimity an aging head of hair."[128] With such an example, I ease the burden of a few gray hairs. To the imperial example of Domitian, I can add a king: Numa Pompilius, second among the Roman kings, was thought to have had gray hair even in his youth. Nor do we lack literary examples. Our Virgil, who we know wrote his *Eclogues* at age twenty-six, was speaking about himself when, through the persona of a shepherd, he said, "when a grayer beard was falling from the razor."[129]

[128]Suetonius, *Lives of the Caesars* VIII, "Domitian," 18.
[129]Virgil, *Eclogues* I, 28.

Augustinus: You certainly have a great cornucopia of examples! If only they were the kind that encouraged you to meditate on death. For I do not approve of examples that show how to disguise the gray that signals either aging or approaching death. For such examples only persuade you to ignore the passage of time and to forget your own inevitable death. Our whole conversation aims to help you remember these things.

But you, when I command you to examine your own gray head, you instead offer a crowd of illustrious gray-haired men. What does that have to do with anything? Only if you could say that these men were immortal would you have, because of their example, a reason not to fear your own gray head. If I had talked about your baldness, I guess you would have trotted out Julius Caesar.

Franciscus: Certainly him and no other. What more illustrious example could I offer? It is a great consolation to be surrounded by such famous companions; and so I confess that I do not reject the use of such examples, which I use as I use the material goods I rely on every day.

For not only in these inconveniences, which either nature or chance have brought my way, but also in those that could befall me, it helps to have something at hand with which I can console myself. And consolation requires either a powerful argument or an outstanding example. If, therefore, you had reproached me because I am afraid of lightning, which I could not deny (this is one reason why I love the laurel tree, which they say is not struck by lightning), I would have responded that Caesar Augustus suffered from the same disease. If you had said that I was blind and this were true, I would have mentioned Appius Caecus and Homer, prince of poets. If you had said "one-eyed," I would have used Hannibal, the Punic leader, or Philip, king of Macedon, as a shield. For "hard of hearing," I would have said Marcus Crassus; for "heat-intolerant," Alexander of Macedon.[130] It would be tedious to go on, but from these examples, you can imagine the others I would give.

---

[130]**Caesar Augustus** (63 B.C.E.–14 C.E.): The first Roman emperor following the rule of Julius Caesar, whose reign had ended the Roman republic. **Appius Caecus:** A Roman leader who in 312 B.C.E. began the construction of the Appian Way, a road that eventually extended from Rome to Brundisium. **Philip:** King of Macedon from 359 to 336 B.C.E. **Marcus Crassus:** A political and military leader in Rome during the first century B.C.E. **Alexander:** Known as Alexander the Great, he succeeded Philip as king of Macedon, ruling until his death in 323 B.C.E. His empire stretched from the Danube to the Indus.

Augustinus: To be honest, this library of examples is fine with me, as long as it doesn't lead to laziness but rather only dispels fear and sorrow. I praise whatever allows you not to fear the coming of old age and not to despise the present. But I detest, I absolutely condemn, whatever suggests that old age does not signal the end of this life and whatever discourages meditation on death. To put it another way, it is a sign of good character if we tolerate prematurely gray hair with good humor and a sense of perspective. But to contrive ways to stave off actual aging—to lie about your own age, to protest that the gray comes too quickly, and to want to hide it or pluck it out—this is, though common enough, the height of dementia.

Do you not see, blind humans, how quickly the stars turn, the stars whose orbit consumes and devours this brief, brief life? Yet still you wonder that old age, brought on by the fleeting course of time, comes to you! There are two things which compel you to this folly: First, that you divide this narrow, contracted life span into even smaller parts, some into four parts—some into six parts, others into even more—as if, not being able to increase the duration of your life, you try to increase it by splitting it into more stages. But what does this dividing game accomplish? Imagine as many stages as you want; in the blink of an eye, all at once, they all pass away. "Not long ago he was born, then a most beautiful baby, now a youth, now a man."[131] Do you see how this most subtle of poets uses the rushing flow of the words to express the passing of a fleeting human life? Thus you try in vain to stretch out what the law of nature, parent of all, has compressed.

The second reason is that you grow old amidst jokes and a false kind of joy. And just as the Trojans, who spent their very last night in such small pleasures, did not anticipate what lay hidden, "while, with one leap, the horse, deadly and loaded down, came over the steep walls of Troy, bearing armed soldiers in its belly," so you are with old age, which carries with it armed and unconquerable death.[132] You do not feel old age as it passes through the walls of your unguarded body until the moment when its soldiers, your enemies, released by rope from their hiding places, "invade the city lying drunk with wine and sleep."[133] For you are no less intoxicated

---

[131] Ovid, *Metamorphoses* X, 522–23.

[132] Virgil, *Aeneid* VI, 515–16.

[133] Ibid., II, 265. Petrarch continues the analogy to Troy by implying the image of the horse and of enemy soldiers emerging from its belly.

by the material existence of the body and the sweet pleasure of temporal things than those whom Virgil intoxicates by wine and sleep. Juvenal speaks eloquently about this: "Like a flower, the brief, fleeting span of our meager and miserable life hurries on, running its course, while we drink; while we demand bouquets, perfumes, and girls, old age steals unnoticed upon us."[134] And so, to get back to the point, do you try to keep out old age when it creeps up and knocks at your door? You argue that, in violation of some law of nature, it has come too soon. When some person who is not old comes along who claims to remember your childhood, you are pleased, especially if he claims that "it seems like only yesterday." You forget that these words can be spoken to anyone, however old and enfeebled. For who is not still a child, no matter how distant from his childhood? Everywhere we see ninety-year-old little boys quarreling over worthless things and even now engrossed in childish preoccupations. The days flow by; the body goes downhill; the soul, it doesn't change. Though everything else starts to rot, the soul never grows up. Indeed, what everyone says is true: One soul uses up many bodies. Childhood flies by, but, as Seneca says, "childishness remains."[135] And believe me, as you yourself have perhaps noticed, you are no longer in childhood. Indeed, most people alive today have not yet grown to be your age.

Therefore, be ashamed to be called an elderly lover. Be ashamed that for so long now you have been the talk of the town. And if the dignity of truly deserved glory doesn't appeal to you, if ignominy doesn't scare you, nonetheless a change in your life now would at least spare your friends the infamy of having to lie on your behalf. And although everyone should accept at least this responsibility, you should be all the more diligent, because you have a large following who are obligated to defend you. "It is a great task to guard a reputation."[136] If in your poem *Africa* you make the fiercest of enemies offer this advice to your Scipio, then allow this pious father to offer the same counsel to you. Leave behind childish follies; extinguish the flames of youth; do not always seek to understand what you have been; observe sometimes what you are. Know that I did not bring up the mirror without cause. Remember what is written in Seneca's *Natural Questions:* "Mirrors were invented so that

[134]Juvenal, *Satires* 9, 126–29.
[135]See Seneca, *Moral Letters to Lucilius* 4, 2.
[136]Petrarch, *Africa* VII, 292.

humans might know themselves. From them, many have acquired a first acquaintance of themselves, then they have gained some insightful advice: beautiful people, to avoid disgrace; ugly ones, that virtue must redeem what the body lacks; young men, that it is time to study and to begin to undertake the tasks of a man; old men, to put aside undignified pursuits when gray hair comes and to meditate a little about death."[137]

Franciscus: I have always remembered that, ever since I first read it. The saying is worth committing to memory, and its counsel is sound.

Augustinus: But what have you gained from having read it and remembered it? Better you should claim the shield of ignorance. For aren't you ashamed to know so much yet to remain, though gray-haired, fundamentally unchanged?

Franciscus: I am ashamed, disgusted, and repentant, but what else can I do? Do you know what brings me comfort? That my beloved grows old along with me.

Augustinus: What has stuck with you, it seems to me, are the words of Julia, the daughter of Caesar Augustus. When her father reprimanded her because she did not enjoy the company of older, serious people, as did her sister Livia, she cleverly retorted, "These serious people will grow old along with me." But do you really think it is more virtuous for you, a senior citizen, to desire an old woman rather than to love a young one? I actually think the opposite: the more worthless the object, the more despicable your passion. Therefore, you should be ashamed—ashamed that your soul never changes, though your body changes relentlessly. And this is all that time allows me to say about shame. As for other arguments, let us seek help from the very source of all remedies, from reason itself, because, as Cicero says, "It is very inappropriate for shame to take the place of reason."[138] And careful reflection, the last of the three things I described when I was discussing what deters a soul from love, will offer that help.

You should know that you are now being called to that high tower, the only place where you can be safe from attacks of passion, because of which you are called "human." Reflect, therefore, above all on the nobility of the soul, which is so great that if I wanted to do it justice, I would have to write an entire book. Reflect at the same time on the fragility and the repulsiveness of the body, a sub-

[137]Seneca, *Natural Questions* I, 17, 4. Petrarch's quotation is not exact.
[138]Cicero, *Tusculan Disputations* II, 21, 47–48.

ject on which the material is equally rich. Reflect on the shortness of life—on this there are books by great men. Reflect on the quick flight of time; there is no one who can adequately describe this in words. Reflect on death—the inevitability of its coming, the uncertainty of its hour, imminent at all times, lurking in all places. Reflect on the one thing that all men deny, because they think they can put off what cannot be put off. For there is no one so unaware of his condition that, if asked, would not acknowledge that sometime or other he is going to die. Therefore, do not let the hope of a longer life, a hope that afflicts many, also mock you. Instead, embrace these words, worthy of a divine oracle: "Believe each day that has dawned to be your last."[139] Why? you ask. Because every day that has shined for mortal creatures is, if not the last, then certainly near to the last.

Think about these things, and also about how vulgar it is to be pointed at and gossiped about. Think about how inconsistent your way of life is with your profession. Think about how much that woman has hurt your soul, your body, and the course of your life. Think about how many trials you have suffered because of her, all for nothing. Think about how many times you have been deceived, despised, and ignored. Think about how many pleading compliments, how many laments, how many tears you have poured out, all into the wind. And at the same time think of *her* haughty and ungrateful disdain! If her manner did ever seem a little kinder, how brief a time this lasted, more ephemeral than a summer breeze. Think about how much you contributed to her reputation yet how much she took from your life. How much you cared for her name, how indifferent she always was to your welfare. Think how far away she took you from the love of God, how many miseries you encountered, miseries that I now pass over in silence, lest I be overheard by someone who happens to hear our conversation.

Think how many activities now surround you to which you might more usefully and more virtuously devote yourself. Think how many incomplete tasks you have on hand, how much better it would be to give these tasks the attention they deserve rather than portioning out to them such a meager share of a mere brief moment. Finally, think about why it is that you want her so ardently. You must really think about this long and hard, like a man, lest perhaps in fleeing, you find yourself more tightly bound, as has

[139] Horace, *Letters* I, 4, 13.

happened to many others, because the sweet memory of her physical beauty creeps in through a tiny opening inside you and this evil is nourished by my remedies. For, among those who have tasted the poison of this irresistible pleasure, there are few who are able to summon either the manliness or the constancy to really consider the filthiness of the female body that I am talking about here. Souls relapse easily, and, as nature urges them on, they return to habits to which they were accustomed and from which they have long suffered.

You must take the utmost care so that this does not happen. Push away all memory of old anxieties. Root out each thought that reminds you of the past, and, as they say, "Dash your children on the rocks," lest, if they rise up, they drag you into the mud.[140] And, at the same time, you must beat down heaven's door with devout prayers, wearing out the ears of the celestial king with pious entreaties. Let no day or night conclude without tears that plead; perhaps the merciful one will put an end to such great suffering. These are the things you must do and the things you must avoid. If you attend to all this with great care, divine help will come, as I hope, and the hand of the invincible liberator will bring you rest.

Although what I have offered is small in comparison to your need, the shortness of time mandates that enough has been said of this one disease. Let us move on to other things. There is one last evil that I must proceed to treat.

Franciscus: Please go on, gentle father, for though I am not yet completely free of these other maladies, I do feel released from the greater part of them.

Augustinus: The glory of men and the immortality of your name mean much more to you than they should. You desire them too much.

Franciscus: You are absolutely right about that. Nor have I been able to find any remedy that curbs this desire.

Augustinus: But this desire should inspire great fear, lest excessive longing for a kind of worthless immortality block your path to true immortality.

Franciscus: I do fear this one thing, among others. I am anxiously waiting to hear from you how I might be made safe, you who have so abundantly supplied remedies for my more serious diseases.

Augustinus: You know that you have no greater disease than this,

---

[140]Psalms 136:9.

though some of the others may be more vile. But what do you imagine this glory that you seek so eagerly is? Explain it.

Franciscus: Are you asking me for a definition? But who knows what this thing is better than you do?

Augustinus: Though the name of glory is known to you, the thing itself, to judge from your actions, is completely foreign. For if you knew what it really was, you would never desire it so ardently. Consider this: Cicero suggested in one place that glory is "a reputation [in Latin *fama*] that is illustrious and widespread either among one's fellow citizens, in one's homeland, or among all of humankind"; or, as he said in another place, glory is "frequent, praising talk *[fama]* about someone."[141] In both cases, you find glory associated with reputation *[fama]*. Do you know what reputation is?

Franciscus: No quick definition comes immediately to mind, and I am afraid to put forth for discussion ideas I am not sure I understand. I prefer to keep my views on this to myself.

Augustinus: This is a prudent and wise course. For in all speech, especially discussion about serious and complex things, attention should be paid not so much to what is said as to what is not said. For the praise one gets for speaking well does not equal the condemnation one suffers for speaking badly. Know, then, that reputation is nothing other than opinions about someone spoken and then spread around by the mouths of the masses.

Franciscus: I praise your definition, or description, if that's what you prefer to call it.

Augustinus: Reputation, therefore, is a kind of blustering or a rush of hot air, and—this you will find even more outrageous—it is the blustering hot air of the majority of people. I know whom I am talking to here. No one has ever thought the mores and the deeds of the masses more hateful than you. Do you now see how perverse your judgments are? You are delighted by the empty little compliments of those whose actual deeds you condemn. Ah, would that you merely delighted in them instead of finding in them the height of your own happiness! For why this endless work of yours, why the late nights, the powerful drive to study? Perhaps you will say that you want to thoroughly understand what will most benefit you in your life. But really, you learned all you need to know about life

---

[141] Cicero, *For Marcellus* 8, 26; perhaps Cicero, *Tusculan Disputations* III, 2, 3.

and death a long time ago. Therefore, you should have tried to put the things you learned into practice rather than persisting in these tedious intellectual exercises, where there are always hidden new abysses to be plumbed, and hidden twists and turns, and where there is no end to the investigation.

Let me add that in those things that please the masses, you have worked even harder, running around in circles trying to please the very people you despise, seizing little pearls of wisdom here from poetry, there from histories, indeed from all kinds of literature, and with these you charm the ears of your listeners.

Franciscus: Excuse me, but I cannot listen to these accusations in silence. Never, not since I was child, have I delighted in little pearls of learning excerpted from other people's books. Rather, I have noted the many things that Cicero eloquently said against these butchers of literature, and above all I have noted that saying of Seneca's: "It is base for a man to pluck such pearls and to prop himself up with famous voices and to stand on what he has memorized."[142]

Augustinus: In saying what I do, I do not reproach you either for laziness or for a bad memory. Instead, I mean to say that out of the books you have read, you have saved up the more dazzling passages for the delight of your comrades; and out of this great heap you have offered the elegant ones for the use of your friends, which is nothing other than pandering for the sake of empty glory. And finally, not content with such ordinary occupations that, although very time-consuming, did not promise great fame beyond the present age, and extending your designs into the future, you sought fame among posterity. And so, reaching out for greater tasks, you began a history of famous men from King Romulus to Emperor Titus, an immense work and one requiring enormous time and effort. And though this huge task was not yet finished (you see how glory spurred you on!), you crossed over to Africa with a poet's pen. Now you concentrate diligently on your poem *Africa,* but without abandoning your history. And so you devote yourself to these two tasks (I pass over all the smaller ones that also intervene), squandering the most valuable of your assets, which, once lost, is gone forever. Writing about others, you forget yourself. How do you know that, with both works unfinished, death will not snatch the exhausted pen from your hand? And so, while you rush around

---

[142]Seneca, *Moral Letters to Lucilius* 33, 7. Petrarch's quotation is not exact.

furiously seeking glory down this twin path, you get what you want from neither.

Franciscus: Sometimes I am afraid of this, I admit. In the grips of a serious illness, I feared that death might be near. And nothing worried me more than that I would leave *Africa* half finished. So, since I rejected the idea of someone else revising it, I had decided to throw it with my own hands into the fire. I trusted no friend to take on this task after my death because I remembered that a similar request made by Virgil was the only one that Augustus refused to honor. And, to make a long story short, it won't take much now for Africa, burned by the flames of the red hot sun, to which it is always subjected, and burned three times by Rome's torches, which laid waste far and wide, to burn again in my flames. But more about this another time. The memory of it is bitter.

Augustinus: Your story confirms my judgment. The day of reckoning has been postponed a little, but the account has not been cleared. For what could be more stupid than to expend such great labor on a thing whose end is uncertain? Still, I know what convinces you — falsely — that a project cannot be abandoned once begun: the hope of finishing it. Since, unless I am wrong, I cannot easily diminish this hope, I will try to strengthen it with my words, so that I can show you how unequal even your great efforts are to this task. Imagine, therefore, that you enjoy ample time, leisure, and quiet; let all intellectual fatigue and physical lassitude fade away. Gone are all the unanticipated obstacles of fortune that, in interrupting the impulse to write, often force down the ready pen. Imagine that all things exceed your happiest dreams. With all of this, what great thing do you think you would accomplish?

Franciscus: Certainly, a great work of extraordinary and rare distinction.

Augustinus: I don't want to be too difficult here. Let's suppose that it is a great work. But if you recognized what an impediment it is to an even greater work, you would abhor what you now desire. I would even say this: In the first place, this great work distracts your soul from all its better duties. Let me add that this great work is not widely known or long-lived; it is contained within the bounds of time and space.

Franciscus: I know this old and trite fable of the philosophers. They say that the whole earth is like a small speck, that a single year consists of an infinite number of years, but that the fame of men does not fill either a speck or a single year. I know this and other stories of this kind, which aim to discourage souls from the love of glory. That said, if you have any arguments that are more persuasive, I'd like to hear them. I have found all these tales to be more specious than efficacious. Nor do I imagine that I can become a god, that I can have eternity, that I can grasp heaven and earth. Human glory is enough for me. This is what I long for. As a mortal, I desire only mortal things.

Augustinus: If this is really what you mean, you are indeed miserable! If you don't desire immortal things, if you don't look for eternity, you are wholly and merely of the earth. Everything is finished for you. No hope of anything more remains.

Franciscus: God keep me from that insanity! My own mind attests that I have *always* burned with a love for eternity. What I said—or if I spoke unclearly, what I meant to say—was this: I use mortal things on behalf of mortal things. I do not, on account of some uncontrolled, insatiable desire, wage war against the ways of nature. Instead, I seek human glory knowing full well that both glory and I are mortal.

Augustinus: This last statement is prudent, but what you said before that is ridiculous. For the sake of a blast of hot air—as you admit, that is meaningless and transitory—you abandon things that endure forever.

Franciscus: I hardly abandon them. I just put them off for a while.

Augustinus: But how dangerous such delaying tactics are in the face of the rush of an uncertain future and the rush of a fleeting life! Just answer me this: If he who alone sets the boundary between life and death would today give you exactly one year of life and this was given to you irrevocably and without any insecurity, how would you begin to allocate that one year?

Franciscus: I would be very stingy and diligent with my time, and I would take the utmost care to spend it only on serious pursuits. Surely, there is no one so insolent or so unsound that they would not give you the same response!

Augustinus: I approve of this answer, but the astonishment that human folly causes me to feel in this matter surpasses not only my powers of speech but also the talents of all who have ever studied eloquence. Although the efforts and the genius of all converge on this one topic, not even their fluency can do it justice.

Franciscus: What is the cause of this astonishment?

Augustinus: Because you are so careful to guard things that are known and certain, while you thoughtlessly waste things that are not certain, when, unless you are completely out of your mind, it ought to be the opposite. This space of a year, although brief, has nonetheless been promised by one who neither deceives nor is deceived and has been given out in parts. Certainly, it could be spent however you please, with only the very last moments reserved for thoughts of your salvation. But it is also truly execrable and horrific dementia to lavish time on ridiculous vanities when you do not know whether the time you have is more than adequate or not enough for the greatest necessities. Whoever has a year to live has something certain, though it is modest. But whoever is under the unpredictable power of death—and this includes all mortals—this person is certain neither of the year, nor of the day, nor of the hour of his death. For someone who has a year, even if six months have gone by, six months still remain. But you, if you lose this day, who can promise you tomorrow? These are the words of Cicero: "It is certain that you must die. It is uncertain whether it will happen today."[143] Nor is anyone so young that "he knows he will make it to evening."[144] Therefore, I ask you, as I ask all mortal creatures who, gazing longingly at the future, do not care for the present: Who knows "whether the gods above will add tomorrow to our lives of today"?[145]

Franciscus: "No one" is, of course, the answer I give on behalf of myself and all mortal creatures. But, as Cicero also said, no one is so old as not to hope for at least another year.[146]

Augustinus: But, as he adds, it is a vain hope not only among the old but also among young people to expect uncertain things as if they were assured. But let's just imagine (although this is altogether impossible) that the duration of your life is known to be ample. Does it not seem demented to you to spend your better years and the best part of your life either in pleasing the eyes of others or in soothing the ears of mortals, and to reserve for God and yourself only the worst and last years, which are good for practically nothing and which only herald the pains and the end of life, so that the freedom of your soul is the care you attend to last? Even if you have all the time you need, doesn't it seem backward to you to postpone the better things?

---

[143]Cicero, *On Old Age* 20, 74.
[144]Ibid., 19, 67. Petrarch's quotation is not exact.
[145]Horace, *Poems* IV, 7, 17–18. Petrarch's quotation is not exact.
[146]Cicero, *On Old Age* 7, 24.

Franciscus: My way of ordering it has a certain rationale. I persuade myself that the glory that it is permitted to hope for here must be sought while I am here. The greater glory is to be enjoyed in heaven; those who get there will have no desire to think about earthly things. And so this is my way: Among mortals, the first care is for mortal things. Eternal things follow transitory ones because it is best to progress from the transitory to the eternal. This is why the way back, from eternal to transitory, is not open.

Augustinus: You are truly an idiot. By that logic, you imagine that all pleasures in heaven or on earth and all the happiest events of both places will flow to you at your command. Indeed, this hope has deceived countless people and has plunged innumerable souls into hell. For while they thought they held one foot here on earth and reached the other up to heaven, in fact they could neither stand here nor ascend to there. They therefore fell miserably, and even though they were in their prime or in the middle of carrying out their business, the spirit of life abandoned them. And this fate, which has befallen so many, do you think it cannot happen to you? If, as you struggle with so many projects, you should—God forbid—suffer ruin, how great the sadness and the shame, and how late the regret will be! Preoccupied by so many things, you will fail at each and every one of them.

Franciscus: I pray to God above that this never happens to me!

Augustinus: Divine mercy might free you from human insanity, but it does not excuse it. I don't want you to hope too much for mercy. For just as God detests those who have given up hope, so he laughs at those who hope without reason. Certainly, I am distressed that you so easily condemn that old fable (as you call it) of the philosophers. For is it then just a fable that depicts, through geometric proofs, the small size of the whole earth and confirms that it is, in fact, a narrow and elongated island? Is it just a fable that asserts that this earth is divided into zones (as they are called)? Does a fable tell us that of these zones, the largest, central one is made uninhabitable by the flames of the sun? That the two on the right and the left are also unable to support human life, oppressed by perpetual cold and ice? And that the two remaining zones, between the central and the outer ones, alone are inhabited? Is it just a fable that locates one of these habitable parts under your feet, inaccessible to you because of the great ocean? You know how much dissension there has long been over the question of whether this part sustains human beings. As for me, I wrote what I think in my book *The City of God,* which no doubt you have read.[147]

The other habitable zone is left to you to live in, or, as some who divide it further into two parts think, one is given to you for your use, and the other is enclosed by the northern ocean and access to it is blocked. Is it an old fable that this part you inhabit, already so small, is diminished by the sea and swamps and woods and beaches and deserts, so that this little piece of earth in which you take such pride is reduced to almost nothing? And finally, is it perhaps an old fable that in this narrow space where you humans live, there are diverse ways of living, conflicting religious practices, dissonant languages, and different habits of dress, and that this severely limits even the potential extent of your fame? If these are only old fables to you, then everything I have told myself about you is also an old fable. For I thought that you understood these things better than practically anyone. Certainly, leaving aside the writings of Cicero and Virgil and other philosophical and poetic teaching — you seem well versed in all of these — I know that recently in your *Africa* you have described these very ideas in outstanding verses. You said, "Confined within narrow bounds, the world is actually a meager island that the ocean surrounds with flowing curves."[148] After this in your poem, you added other similar things. If you thought these were just false fables, I am surprised that you repeated them so often. Why now should I speak of the brevity of mortal fame and the fleeting nature of the temporal realm when you know how short-lived even our oldest memory of greatness is when compared to eternity? I do not here refer you to the opinions of the ancients, who warn of frequent fires and floods on earth. Both Plato's *Timaeus* and the sixth book of Cicero's *On the Republic* abound with these opinions. And, although they seem more or less probable to many, these opinions mean something altogether different to the true religion to which you belong.

But, leaving all this aside, look how many things there are that impede the survival of a name for a long time, let alone for eternity. In the first place, there is the death of those with whom one has

[147] See *The City of God* XVI, 9, where Augustine disputes the idea that there are clear and compelling reasons for believing that the "other" side of the earth — that is, the side opposite the Mediterranean world — is inhabited by human beings.

[148] Petrarch, *Africa* II, 361–63.

lived one's life. There is forgetfulness, a natural disease of old age. And there is growing praise for new, younger men, which as it flourishes detracts significantly from longer established glory and seems to rise up higher the more it suppresses praise for older men. With this competition comes envy, which relentlessly follows those seeking glory. Then there is the hatred of virtue and the contempt that the crowd feels for the life of the mind. Add to this the uncertainty of popular judgment. Add the decay of tombs, which can be shattered, as Juvenal said, "by the evil strength of a sterile fig branch."[149] In your *Africa,* you elegantly called this "a second death." And so, if I might here address you in the same words that there you made another speak, "Soon the bust will lie in ruins, and the inscribed marble will fall in shattered stone; from this, my son, you will suffer a second death."[150] This is bright and immortal glory, this glory that totters at the blow of a single stone? Add the destruction of books in which your name has been written either by your own or another's hand. Although the memory of books lasts longer than that of tombs, and thus books seem longer-lived, their destruction nonetheless is inevitable, because of the innumerable calamities of nature and fortune alike, to which books, like everything else, are subject. And even if books were to avoid all these, still old age and mortality doom them. "For it is fitting that all things produced through the small genius of mortal labor are themselves also mortal."[151] Thus may your own words powerfully refute your childish error. Let me continue to treat you with your own verses: "Certainly, you yourself will fall again as your books perish. For you, there remains this third death."[152] There you have my judgment concerning glory expressed, certainly in more words than is appropriate for you or me, but in fewer words than the matter itself demands—unless perhaps to you this all seems like just more old fables.

Franciscus: Not at all! Nor did your words affect my soul only as fables do, but rather they have inspired in me a new desire to cast out old habits. For, although almost all these things have long been known to me and I have often heard them, because, as our Terence said, "nothing is now said that hasn't already been said," nonetheless the

[149]Juvenal, *Satires* 10, 145.
[150]Petrarch, *Africa* II, 431–32.
[151]Ibid., 455–57.
[152]Ibid., 464–65.

dignity of the words and the order of your account and the authority of the one speaking carry a lot of weight.[153] Now I would like you to clarify your last word on the subject: Do you want me to put all my studies aside to live in obscurity, without glory, or do you advise some compromise?

Augustinus: I would never advise you to live without glory, but I do repeatedly admonish you not to prefer the desire for glory to the desire for virtue. For you know that glory is virtue's shadow; just as it is impossible for the body not to produce a shadow when struck by the sun, so virtue cannot help but produce glory wherever God shines on it. Therefore, whoever abolishes true glory has necessarily already abolished virtue. And with virtue abolished, human life is left naked, identical to that of mute animals, driven by the call of appetite, which is the only love beasts have.

Let this, therefore, be the law that you follow: Honor virtue; do not worry about its shadow glory. For, as Cato [the Elder] is said to have remarked, the less you seek it, the more you attain it. I am still unable to resist quoting your own words to you: "Although you, unwilling, flee, this follows you."[154] Do you recognize this verse? You wrote it.

Think of it this way: Surely, only a lunatic would run around sweating at midday in the heat of the sun so that he could see his shadow and show it to others. Well, the person is no saner who hauls himself around in the heat of life so that he can spread his own fame and glory. What then? Let each one go toward the goal he has set for himself; his shadow follows him wherever he goes. Let him pursue what he understands as virtue; glory will not abandon him. This is what I think about glory, which is the companion of true virtue. The kind of name recognition that is sought through other arts, both physical and mental—and human ingenuity invents innumerable of these—is not worthy of the name of glory.

As for you, who make yourself sick by working so hard to write books, if I may say so, especially given your age, you are far off the right track. Having forgotten your own self, you attend wholeheartedly to the affairs of others. And as you strive after an inane kind of glory, your brief life is wasted, and you don't even realize it.

---

[153]Terence, *The Eunuch,* prologue, 41.
[154]For the reference to Cato the Elder, see Sallust, *The Conspiracy of Cataline* 54, 3; Petrarch, *Africa* II, 486.

Franciscus: What should I do then? Should I abandon my efforts midstream? Wouldn't it be wiser to work more quickly and, if God allows it, to put the final touches on them, so that, divested of these cares, I might move on more expediently to greater ones? For I cannot easily abandon in the middle of the journey such a great and extravagant work.

Augustinus: I see now why you are dragging your feet. You would rather abandon yourself than your books. I will press my case. To what end I do so remains to be seen, but certainly I do it in good faith. Lay down the great burdens of history. The deeds of the Romans have been sufficiently depicted both by their own reputation and through the ingenuity of others. Abandon Africa and leave it to its possessors, for there you will acquire no glory, either for Scipio or for yourself. Scipio could not be extolled more highly than he already is, and you are only struggling behind him on an indirect path.

Once these things have been put in their place, then finally return yourself to yourself and, to come back to the main point of our discussion, begin to think about death, which you slowly and unknowingly are approaching. Rip off the veil. Dispel the darkness. Fix your eyes on death alone. Beware lest a single day or night pass by that does not compel you to reflect upon your final hour. Whatever you see, whatever you think about, interpret it in light of this one thing. The sky, the earth, the ocean all change; what can humans, the most fragile of creatures, hope for?

The changes of time run their course; nothing stays the same. If you think that you can avoid change, you are dead wrong. But, as Horace said so elegantly, "though swift moons repair heavenly damage, we fall where we may."[155]

Therefore, whenever you see the summer corn follow spring flowers, or a temperate autumn follow the heat of summer, whenever you see winter snow follow autumn harvests, say to yourself, "Although the seasons pass away, they will always return. I, however, depart forever." Whenever in the evening you notice the shadows of the mountains growing longer as the sun sets, say, "Now, as life flees, the shadow of death stretches out. The sun will rise again tomorrow, but for me this day is gone forever."

Who can describe the spectacular beauty of a serene night, which is both the most opportune time for those doing evil and the

[155]Horace, *Poems* IV, 7, 13–14.

most devout time for those doing good? For this reason, be like the master of the Trojan fleet. The strait you sail is no safer than the one he navigated. Rise up, as he did, in the middle of the night and "note all the stars gently turning in the quiet sky."[156] And when you see these stars hurry to the west, know that you are pushed along with them and that no hope of remaining exists save the hope you have in one who never moves nor falls. Further, when you meet people now whom you saw as children, people who are year by year growing up, remember that, as they grow, you are going down the other side of life, and faster since our inferior nature makes all falls heavier.

Let the sight of an ancient building make you think, "Where are the people whose hands built this?" When you see a newer building, think, "Where will those who built this soon be?" Ask yourself similar questions about trees. The one who planted and cultivated a tree is often not the one who picks the fruit from its branches. Indeed, in many things, that line from Virgil's *Georgics* applies: "The tree comes late to make shade for your distant descendants."[157] A certain line of yours might be cited here (lest I always refer you to others) if you are marveling at swiftly rushing waters: "Certainly no river flows a course at a speed swifter than that at which the time of a human life passes."[158] Do not be fooled by the great number of days and the laborious division of time into small units. The whole life of a human being, however long it lasts, seems like a single day, and even then hardly a whole one. Hold constantly before your eyes the comparison made by Aristotle, which I have noticed greatly pleases you and which deeply moves the spirit every time it is read or heard. You will find Aristotle's analogy retold more eloquently and more persuasively by Cicero in the *Tusculan Disputations,* either in these exact words or words very similar (I don't have the book at hand). Cicero says, "Along the river Hypanis, Aristotle writes, which flows from the coast of Europe into the Black Sea, certain little animals are born who live for one day. One of these who dies in the morning dies young. If one dies at midday, it dies a bit further along. But the one who dies at night dies old. And this is all the more true if the day is a solstice. Compare the whole expanse of our existence with eternity, and we find that we are in

[156]Virgil, *Aeneid* III, 515.

[157]Virgil, *Georgics* II, 58.

[158]Petrarch, *Metrical Epistles* I, 4, 91–92.

nearly the same situation as these little animals."[159] I think that this assertion is so true that from the mouths of philosophers, it has long since spread to everyone. For surely you have noticed that uneducated, unknowing people have adopted this image in their everyday speech, so that when they see a child they say, "For this one, it is morning." And when they see an adult, they say, "It is midday or afternoon for this one." But when they see an old, decrepit person, they say, "This one arrives at evening; the sun is setting." My dearest child, consider these things and any similar thoughts that come to you—no doubt there are many. The ones I have described are just those that at this time have suggested themselves.

I ask one more thing of you: Contemplate diligently the tombs of those older persons whom you have known. Know that the same resting place and eternal home awaits you. "All of us move toward this place. Here is the last home of everyone."[160] You too, who now, in the full bloom of life, arrogantly walk upon the dead, will soon yourself be underfoot. Think about these things; meditate on them day and night, not only as befits a serious human being mindful of his nature but also as befits a philosopher. In this way, you will be able to understand what is written: "The whole life of a philosopher is careful preparation for death."[161] This thought, I say, will teach you to scorn mortal achievements and will show you another way to live, one you must seize with both hands. Now you ask me what this way is, or through which paths one might arrive at it. And I will answer that you do not need detailed directions. All you need to do is listen to your spirit calling out and constantly exhorting you, saying, "This is the way home." You know what this spirit suggests to you; you know which paths and detours it recommends that you follow, which it recommends that you avoid. Obey the voice of your spirit if you desire to be safe and free. Lengthy deliberation is not necessary here. Rather, the immediacy of the danger demands action. The enemy assaults you on all sides. The walls tremble around you. You cannot hesitate any longer. What good is it to sing sweetly for others if you do not listen to yourself? I must conclude: Avoid the rocks. Pull yourself away and into safety. Follow the passion of your spirit, which, although it is base when turned toward

---

[159]Cicero, *Tusculan Disputations* I, 39, 94.
[160]See Ovid, *Metamorphoses* X, 34.
[161]Cicero, *Tusculan Disputations* I, 30, 74.

other things, is when turned towards virtuous things as beautiful as it could be.

Franciscus: If only you had told me these things from the beginning, before I committed myself to my studies.

Augustinus: I did say these things to you, and often. And in the very beginning, when I saw you had taken up your pen, I warned that life would be brief and uncertain, while your labor would surely be long. The work you undertook would be enormous, the fruit only meager. But the cheers of the crowd had blocked your ears — cheers that, to my horror, you both hated and followed. For the rest, since we have talked for long enough, I ask you this: If you have found something pleasing in my words, do not allow yourself to pine away in laziness and inertia. If, however, I have been too harsh, do not take it badly.

Franciscus: Not to worry — I am very grateful to you for many things and especially for these three days of conversation, because you have cleared my blurred vision and you have dispelled the dense cloud of error that swirled around me. And what great thanks I owe to Truth, who, not troubled by our extensive talk, has stayed with us until the end. For if she had averted her gaze, we would have wandered aimlessly in the dark, far from the right path, and your words would have held no clear meaning, nor would my intellect have been able to make use of them.

But now your place is in heaven, whereas my time on earth is not yet finished. I do not know how long my life will last, and, as you see, this uncertainty makes me anxious. Please, I ask you, please do not desert me, though I am very far away. For without you, dearest father, my life is bleak, and without Truth, I could not live at all.

Augustinus: Imagine your prayer already answered; only see that you do not desert yourself. If you do, you will justly be abandoned by everyone.

Franciscus: I will attend to myself as far as I am able. I will collect the scattered fragments of my soul, and I will diligently focus on myself alone. But now, even as we speak, many other obligations, though admittedly mortal ones, still await me.

Augustinus: Perhaps these other things seem very important to the great majority. However, certainly there is nothing more useful and there is nothing that could yield more fruit than a focus on yourself. These other claims on you, mortal things, might prove empty, but your inevitable end, which is death, demonstrates the necessity of attending to oneself.

Franciscus: I know. The only reason I am now so eager to fulfill my other obligations is so that once these are completed, I can return to the care of myself and my soul. I know, as you said a little while ago, that it would be much safer for me to pursue only the care of myself now and, bypassing the detours, to seize the right path of salvation. But I cannot restrain my desire for the world.

Augustinus: This is our old argument. What you call inability is really a question of will. But let it go; we cannot ever agree. I pray that God goes with you wherever you go, even when you stray, and that by his command you arrive safely.

Franciscus: How I hope that your prayer comes true, so that, with God leading, I can safely avoid all detours and, as I follow the one who calls me, I don't kick up dust into my own eyes. I hope that the turmoil in my soul subsides, that the call of the world is silent, and that Fortune does not rage against me.

PART THREE

Related Documents

These brief texts illustrate some aspects of Petrarch's humanism that are important for understanding the structure and composition of *The Secret*. They particularly highlight Petrarch's intensely personal relationship with the ancients (see the first selection) and the disjunction between Petrarch's Augustinus and the historical Augustine (the second and third selections).

PETRARCH

First Letter to Marcus Tullius Cicero
Dated June 16, 1345

Petrarch devoted much time and energy to compiling and editing his correspondence for publication. One of these collections, known as the Familiar Letters, *contains several letters to ancient authors, including two to Cicero. The first of these, which appears here, is dated June 16, 1345—that is, shortly after Petrarch discovered a manuscript in a library in Verona containing a group of Cicero's personal letters. Of*

Petrarch, *Familiar Letters* XXIV, 3. Translated by Carol E. Quillen.

particular importance to Petrarch were the hundreds of letters that Cicero wrote to his lifelong confidant and political ally Atticus. As boys, Cicero and Atticus attended school together, but sometime around 86 B.C.E., Atticus left Rome for Athens, where he lived for the next twenty years. Although Atticus returned to Rome in about 65 B.C.E., he continued to spend much of his time in Epirus (the northwestern part of Greece).

Throughout his tumultuous legal and political career, which spanned the violent transition in Rome from republic to empire, Cicero relied on Atticus for candid advice and support. His letters dramatically illustrate his ambition and fears, his political strategizing, his arm-twisting and backstabbing, his ever-shifting alliances, and his sometimes glaringly bad judgment. Above all, Cicero's letters to Atticus attest to the dangerous instability and the profound uncertainty that characterized political life in Rome during the last half of the first century B.C.E.

The letter reprinted here communicates something of the excitement that Petrarch and other humanists felt as they encountered lost or ignored classical texts and as they used those texts to imagine and reconstruct the personalities who wrote them. Because Petrarch was interested not only in the teachings of ancient texts but also in the personalities of ancient authors, his letter expresses dismay at what he takes to be Cicero's weaknesses. Indeed, there are some similarities between Petrarch's criticisms of Cicero here and the criticisms that Augustinus makes of Franciscus in The Secret. *This letter also reveals Petrarch's scorn for politics, an attitude not shared by his humanist successors.*

As you read the letter, ask yourself why Petrarch is so upset with Cicero. What exactly is his lament? What kinds of examples does he cite? Why does he end the letter the way he does?

Franciscus sends greetings to his Cicero. Your letters—which I long sought and then found where I least expected—I have now read voraciously.[1] I have heard you, Marcus Tullius, speaking about many things, lamenting many things, and equivocating about many things. I who have known for a long time what kind of a teacher you were to others now finally see who you were to yourself.

---

[1]My translation of this letter is from the Latin text in Francesco Petrarca, *Familiarium Rerum Libri,* ed. Vittorio Rossi and Umberto Bosco (Florence, 1933–41), 4: 225–27. My notes on this text derive from the ones in that edition.

Wherever you are, you in turn hear this, which is not advice but rather a lament, born of genuine concern, that one of your descendants who dearly loves your name now offers. O restless and distressed one, or, to use words you can recognize as your own, "O rash and miserable old man,"[2] why did you commit yourself to so many contentious struggles and to rivalries utterly without benefit? Why did you give up the dignified and detached way of life that so suited your age, your profession, and your history? What false gleam of glory pulled you, an old man, into the fights of boys and pushed you on, through all kinds of tumultuous misfortunes, to a death unworthy of a philosopher? Alas, unmindful of the advice of your brother, unmindful of so many of your own sound precepts, you, like a nighttime traveler carrying the light, showed your followers the path on which you yourself pathetically stumbled.

I leave aside Dionysius, I leave aside your brother and your nephew, and, if you like, I even leave aside Dolabella, all men whom you praise to the sky at one moment and tear to shreds with sudden outbursts the next.[3] Perhaps these examples may be excused. I also pass over Julius Caesar, whose famed compassion was a refuge for those who threatened him. I do not speak about the great Pompey, with whom you, through the power of friendship, seemed capable of accomplishing whatever you liked.[4] But what madness drove you

---

[2]Petrarch is alluding to a phrase from the pseudo-Ciceronian *Letter to Octavianus* (the adopted name of Octavius [in English, sometimes called Octavian], whom we now know as Caesar Augustus, the first emperor of Rome). Petrarch discovered this letter, which he took to be authentic, along with genuine ones written by and to Cicero in 1345.

[3]The men mentioned in this portion of the letter all figure prominently in Cicero's correspondence. Dionysius (Pomponius Dionysius) was a former servant of Atticus and the tutor to Cicero's son. Early on in the correspondence, Cicero speaks very highly of him, but later he expresses frustration at Dionysius's lack of loyalty and gratitude. Dolabella (Publius Cornelius Dolabella) was a savvy but somewhat irresponsible man whom Cicero defended twice in court. Dolabella married Tullia, Cicero's daughter, over Cicero's objections. They later divorced. Although Dolabella supported Julius Caesar until his assassination, afterward he negotiated with those who had killed him. Eventually, Dolabella alienated powerful members of the senate in Rome, and as he was about to be captured, he committed suicide.

[4]Cicero and Pompey became friends and political allies because both distrusted another politician named Marcus Crassus. Later, Julius Caesar, Pompey, and Crassus joined forces as the First Triumvirate. Cicero thought that this alliance violated the constitution of the republic. Pompey and Cicero later clashed over the best way to defeat Caesar, who had become dictator. Caesar was assassinated in 44 B.C.E. Brutus was one of the conspirators.

against Antony? I guess it was love for the republic—the republic that you admitted had already completely collapsed. And even if it were pure faith, even if the idea of liberty compelled you, why then this great friendship with Augustus? Indeed, how will you respond to your Brutus? He said, "If you so like Octavius,[5] you seem not to have fled a master but to have sought a friendlier one."[6] One thing remained, unhappy Cicero, and this was your last senseless battle. You cursed this very man whom you had so praised not because he was doing you any harm but because he was unable to stop those who were.

I grieve, my friend, at your inconsistency. I am ashamed and distressed by your errors. And now, with this same Brutus, "I grant nothing to these arts in which I know that you were expert."[7] For really, what good is it to teach others, of what benefit is it to speak constantly about virtues, using the most elegant words, if at the same time you yourself don't hear your words? How much more fitting it would have been, especially for a philosopher, to have grown old in the peaceful countryside, thinking, as you yourself wrote someplace,[8] not about this meager life but about the one that endures; how much more fitting it would have been had you held no office, had you panted after no victories, had no Catilines[9] inflated your spirit. But I say these things in vain. Farewell forever, my Cicero.

Written among the living, on the right bank of the river Adige, in the city of Verona, in Transpadane Italy, on June 16th in the 1345th year from the birth of the God you never knew.

---

[5]"Octavius" and "Augustus" refer to the same person, Caesar Augustus, the first Roman emperor. For a time, Cicero thought that he could use Octavius against Marc Antony, who seized power after Julius Caesar's assassination. He was wrong. After Antony, Octavius, and Lepidus formed the Second Triumvirate, Cicero was executed.

[6]This line comes from a letter Brutus wrote to Cicero, preserved in Cicero's *Letters to Brutus,* 16, 7.

[7]From a letter that Brutus wrote to Atticus, one of Cicero's closest friends, in Cicero, *Letters to Brutus,* 17, 5.

[8]Petrarch is referring to Cicero's *Letters to Atticus,* 8, 8.

[9]**Catiline:** Lucius Sergius Catilina (fl. ca. 60 B.C.E.) was the leader of a failed plot to overthrow the Roman government in 63 B.C.E. Cicero helped to expose the plot.

AUGUSTINE

From *Confessions*

Finished ca. 400 C.E.

Readers of The Secret *have long recognized the differences between the Augustinus of Petrarch's dialogue and the historical Augustine. These differences emerge starkly in the first dialogue, where Augustinus insists that humans can shed their unhappiness through an act of will: If their will is strong enough, they will obtain what they desire. Later in the first dialogue, Augustinus represents his own conversion as described in the* Confessions *as an act of will: When his will was sufficiently strong, he was able to convert. Comparing Augustinus's account of his conversion with the following passage from the* Confessions *shows that Petrarch, who was too careful a reader to have misunderstood Augustine, intended for Augustinus to be different from his historical namesake. Whereas Augustinus attributes his conversion to the power of his will, Augustine sees his ability to convert as a gift from God. Although there are many possible explanations for this and other discrepancies, the introduction to this volume argues that Petrarch wanted to create Augustinus in such a way that Augustinus could authorize humanist activities as redemptive.*

In this excerpt, Alypius is a friend of Augustine's who was sitting nearby, and Antony is Anthony of Egypt (ca. 251–356 C.E.), one of the earliest Christian hermits who withdrew from human society to lead a solitary ascetic life.

Then, from deep within, a profound reflection dragged up and brought together all of my misery "for my heart to see,"[1] and there arose within me a huge storm bearing a huge shower of tears. And I stood up and moved away from Alypius so that I could let my tears flow without stifling the sobs (solitude seemed more fitting to me for the task of crying) and I withdrew far enough away from him for his presence not to burden me. I was very upset, and he sensed this. I think I had said something, I am not sure what, in which the sound of my

[1]Psalms 18:15.

Augustine, *Confessiones* VIII, 12, 28–29. *Corpus Christianorum Series Latina* XXVII (Turnhout: Brepols, 1981). Translated by Carol E. Quillen.

voice had betrayed my weeping, and so I had moved away. He [Alypius] therefore remained where we had been sitting, astonished at my state. I somehow threw myself to the ground under a certain fig tree, and let loose my flood of tears, and rivers flowed from my eyes, a sacrifice acceptable to you,[2] and I said to you (not in these exact words but with this meaning), "Oh, Lord, for how long? For how long, Lord, will your anger know no bounds? Do not be mindful of our old iniquities."[3] For I felt that I was held back by these. I hurled out in a miserable voice, "How long, how long will it be tomorrow and tomorrow? Why not now? Why not an end to my sinful life right at this moment?"

I was saying these things and crying, my heart in bitter agony. And suddenly from a house nearby I hear a voice singing—a boy or a girl, I don't know—saying and repeating over and over, "Pick it up and read, pick it up and read." At once my demeanor changed, and I began to think very intently if there was some game in which children usually sang in this way. I did not think I had heard of one. Forcing back my tears, I stood up, understanding that the child's voice could only be divine and that it commanded me to open a book and to read the first chapter that I found. For I had heard that when Saint Antony had by chance been present at a gospel reading, he took the admonition that was read as if it were directed at him: "Go, sell all that you have and give it to the poor, and you will have riches in heaven; and come, follow me."[4] And by this oracle he was immediately converted to you. And so awakened, I returned to the place where Alypius was sitting, to where I had put down the book of the Apostle [that is, a book of Paul's letters] when I had stood up. I snatched it up, I opened it, and I read to myself the verse that first struck my eyes: "Not in carousing and drinking parties, not in bedrooms and lewd behavior, not in competition and rivalry; rather put on the Lord Jesus Christ and do not provide for the flesh and its desires."[5] I did not want to read further, nor was there any need, because as soon as I finished this sentence every shadow of doubt evaporated, as if my heart had been infused with the light of certainty.

[2]See Psalms 50:19.
[3]See Psalms 6:4.
[4]Matthew 19:21.
[5]Romans 13:13–14.

VIRGIL

From *Aeneid*

ca. 20 B.C.E.

and

AUGUSTINE

From *The City of God*

Finished ca. 426 C.E.

In The Secret, *Augustinus relies heavily on the words of the ancients as he tries to help Franciscus. Indeed, the dialogue suggests that reading pagan texts is central to the quest for human happiness and salvation. This argument about the redemptive power of ancient literature was an important part of Renaissance humanism and it endured well into the modern era. Yet it is an argument that the historical Augustine never made.*

Augustine lived under the Roman Empire during the fourth and fifth centuries. Like most educated men of his day, he grew up steeped in the works of Cicero and Virgil. His writings therefore recall and refer to the ancient authors whom Petrarch most admired. For Petrarch, Augustine's life and work provided evidence that he did not have to choose between the ancient pagan texts he loved and Christianity. Why should he reject the very authors whom he finds in the writings of a venerable church father? If a towering Christian figure like Augustine read and quoted Virgil, then surely so could he.[1]

Augustine did indeed refer extensively to pagan authors in his writings, especially in The City of God. *In this sense he resembles Petrarch's Augustinus, who also cites these authors. However, whereas Augustinus most often cites ancient pagan texts to show how they can help Franciscus in his search for Christian happiness, the historical Augustine often cites ancient pagan texts to show how different they are from Christian*

---

[1]See Petrarch, *Familiar Letters* II, 9.

Virgil, *Aeneid* Book VI, lines 965–1013. Translated by Robert Fitzgerald (New York: Vintage Books, 1983), 185–86.

Augustinus, Aurelius. *De Civitate Dei* XIV, 3. *Corpus Christianorum Series Latina* XLVIII (Turnhout: Brepols, 1955). Translated by Carol E. Quillen.

teaching. He wrote The City of God <u>*against the pagans, as a celebration*</u> *of a specifically Christian outlook.*

The passage given here shows how differently Petrarch's Augustinus and the historical Augustine used the same passage from Virgil's Aeneid. *The* Aeneid *recounts the adventures of Aeneas, a Trojan hero, from the end of the Trojan War, during which the Greeks had destroyed the city of Troy, to his arrival at the site where Rome will be founded. The quotation comes from Book VI. At this point in the poem, Aeneas has traveled to Elysium (the region of the underworld where good souls go after death) with a Sybil as his guide. Here he meets his father, Anchises. Aeneas asks his father whether souls return from Elysium to earth, and Anchises then explains how souls enter bodies, live on earth, die, and sometimes live on earth again. Augustinus and Augustine quote lines that correspond to lines 981–987 of this translation. Compare Augustine's interpretation below with that of Augustinus on pages 68–69. Note that both disregard the context of the quotation from Virgil.*

Aeneid

965   "Must we imagine,
        Father, there are souls that go from here
        Aloft to upper heaven, and once more
        Return to bodies' dead weight? The poor souls,
        How can they crave our daylight so?"
970   "My son,
        I'll tell you, not to leave you mystified,"
        Anchises said, and took each point in order:

973   First, then, the sky and lands and sheets of water,
        The bright moon's globe, the Titan sun and stars,
975   Are fed within by Spirit, and a Mind
        Infused through all the members of the world
        Makes one great living body of the mass.
        From Spirit come the races of man and beast,
        The life of birds, odd creatures the deep sea
980   Contains beneath her sparkling surfaces,
        And fiery energy from a heavenly source
        Belongs to the generative seeds of these,
        So far as they are not poisoned or clogged

By mortal bodies, their free essence dimmed
985 By earthiness and deathliness of flesh.
This makes them fear and crave, rejoice and grieve.
Imprisoned in the darkness of the body
They cannot clearly see heaven's air; in fact
Even when life departs on the last day
990 Not all the scourges of the body pass
From the poor souls, not all distress of life.
Inevitably, many malformations,
Growing together in mysterious ways,
Become inveterate. Therefore they undergo
995 The discipline of punishments and pay
In penance for old sins: some hang full length
To the empty winds, for some the stain of wrong
Is washed by floods or burned away by fire.
We suffer each his own shade. We are sent
1000 Through wide Elysium, where a few abide
In happy lands, till the long day, the round
Of Time fulfilled, has worn our stains away,
Leaving the soul's heaven-sent perception clear,
The fire from heaven pure. These other souls,
1005 When they have turned Time's wheel a thousand years,
The god calls in a crowd to Lethe stream,
That there unmemoried they may see again
The heavens and wish re-entry into bodies."
Anchises paused. He drew both son and Sibyl
1010 Into the middle of the murmuring throng,
Then picked out a green mound from which to view
The souls as they came forward, one by one,
1014 And to take note of faces.

The City of God

The cause of sin came from the soul, not from the flesh, and the degeneration that results from sin is not itself a sin but a punishment for sin.

Now, if someone says that, in the sphere of bad morals, the flesh is the cause of every kind of vice, because the influence of the body makes the soul live in this bad way, then surely that person has not carefully considered the whole of human nature. It is true that "the corruptible body aggravates the soul."[1] And for this reason, when speaking about this subject, the Apostle Paul said, "Yes, our outer selves are degenerating."[2] Yet he goes on to say about the corruptible body: "We know that if our earthly dwelling place is destroyed, we have a building from God, a house not made by hands, but rather an eternal house in heaven. Indeed, in this earthly dwelling place we groan, longing for it to be clothed with our heavenly home, hoping that, if it is so clothed, we will not be found naked. For we who are here in this earthly dwelling groan under its weight. Yet we do not want to be stripped of this shelter, but rather to have the other put on over it, so that what is mortal can be absorbed by life."[3]

And so although we are weighed down by the corruptible body, we know that the cause of this oppression is not the nature or the materiality of the body, but its degeneration. Thus we do not want to be stripped of the body but we want it to be clothed with its immortality. For then there will still be a body, but it will not be subject to degeneration. For now "the corruptible body weighs down the soul, and earthly existence presses in on the mind, which is taking in many things."[4] Still, those who think that all afflictions of the soul have arisen from the body are wrong.

It is true that Virgil seems to be using splendid poetry to explain Platonic teaching when he says, "Fiery energy and a heavenly origin dwell within those generative seeds [of living creatures], to the degree that they are not impeded by poisonous bodies or dulled by limbs of the flesh."[5] Here Virgil wants us to understand that all four of the best-known disturbances of the soul—desire, fear, happiness, and grief—which are as it were the origins of all vice, arise from the body. He thus then adds: "From this they fear and desire, they grieve and rejoice. Enclosed in a pitch-black prison, they do not see the heavens."[6] Nonetheless, our [Christian] faith asserts something very different. For the degeneration of the body that weighs down the soul is not the cause of the first sin, but rather its punishment. And the corruptibility of the flesh does not make the soul a sinner, but rather the sinful soul makes the flesh corruptible.

---

[1] Wisdom 9:15. Augustine's rendition of this biblical passage differs slightly from Petrarch's in *The Secret*.
[2] 2 Corinthians 4:16.
[3] 2 Corinthians 5:1–4.
[4] Wisdom 9:15.
[5] Virgil, *Aeneid* VI, 730–32.
[6] Ibid., 733–34.

Glossary of Names

Aeneas   In mythology, a great Trojan leader and hero of Virgil's *Aeneid.*

Aeolus   Greek mythological king; "Keeper of the Winds."

Alexander   Alexander the Great (356–323 B.C.E.); Alexander III of Macedon; pupil of Aristotle whose empire stretched from the Danube to the Indus.

Amphion of Thebes   Greek mythological figure known for his talent as a musician.

Apollo   Greek god of light, youth, beauty, prophecy, music, and poetry.

Aristotle   (384–322 B.C.E.) Greek philosopher, student of Plato, head of Lyceum, and tutor of Alexander the Great; his philosophical works were the foundation for much medieval scholastic thought.

Augustine   (354–430 C.E.) Latin church father, author of the *Confessions,* and bishop of Hippo; inspiration for the interlocutor Augustinus.

Augustus, Caesar   (63 B.C.E.–14 C.E.) First Roman emperor following rule of Julius Caesar.

Bacchus   Ancient god of the productive capacity of plants in nature who became associated especially with wine; also called Dionysus.

Barlaam   (ca. 1290–1350 C.E.) Calabrian Basilian monk who facilitated the study of the Greek language in the early Renaissance; Petrarch briefly studied Greek with him.

Bellerophon   Hero of Greek legend; Homer recounts how Bellerophon, after a lifetime filled with tragedy and Herculean challenges, eventually incurred the wrath of the gods and was left to wander, grief-stricken and alone.

Boethius   Anicius Manlius Severinus Boethius (ca. 480–524 C.E.); philosopher and Christian theologian who wrote treatises on logic, arithmetic, music, and theology; his dialogue *Consolation of Philosophy* influenced Petrarch's *The Secret.*

Brutus   Marcus Junius Brutus (ca. 85–42 B.C.E.); Roman politician and one of Julius Caesar's assassins.

Caecus, Appius   Appius Claudius Caecus (fl. ca. 300 B.C.E.); early Roman statesman who began construction of the Appian Way in 312 B.C.E..

Caesar, Julius   (102–44 B.C.E.) Roman general, statesman, and historian whose reign as dictator marked the end of the Roman republic.

Cato the Elder   Marcus Porcius Cato or Cato the Elder (234–149 B.C.E.); Roman politician and a central figure in the Third Punic War against Carthage; author of the oldest extant Latin prose text, a treatise on farming.

Cato the Younger   Marcus Porcius Cato or Cato the Younger (95–46 B.C.E.); Roman politician, contemporary of Cicero, and staunch defender of the Roman republic against Julius Caesar.

Cicero   Marcus Tullius Cicero (106–43 B.C.E.); Roman orator, statesman, and philosopher.

Cimber   L. Tillius Cimber (fl. ca. 50 B.C.E.); one of the conspirators in the assassination of Julius Caesar.

Crassus, Marcus   Marcus Licinius Crassus (ca. 115–53 B.C.E.); Roman politician who along with Julius Caesar and Pompey formed the First Triumvirate, an informal political alliance that governed Rome just before the civil wars that led to the autocratic reign of Julius Caesar.

Daphne   In Greek mythology, the daughter of a river god; she fled Apollo's advances and was turned into a laurel tree to prevent him from capturing her.

Dido   The legendary founder of the city of Carthage; also called Elissa. Although the common date for the fall of Troy is centuries earlier, in the *Aeneid* Virgil presents Dido and the Trojan hero Aeneas as contemporaries. Dido falls in love with Aeneas and commits suicide when he leaves Carthage to found Rome.

Dis   Roman god of the underworld; equivalent to the Greek god Hades or Pluto; also called Orcus.

Domitian   Titus Flavius Domitianus (51–96 C.E.); emperor of Rome 81–96 C.E.; his reign is noted for its severity, especially in the terror of 93–96 C.E.

Eurydice   In Greek mythology, the wife of Orpheus.

Furies   Three Greek and Roman goddesses of vengeance who lived in the underworld.

Gellius, Aulus   (ca. 123–165 C.E.) Roman author who wrote the *Attic Nights*.

Hades   Greek god of the underworld; equivalent to the Roman god Dis; also called Pluto or Pluton.

Hannibal   (ca. 247–181 B.C.E.) Carthaginian general and enemy of Rome who provoked the Second Punic War; defeated by Scipio Africanus.

Helen In Greek legend, the most beautiful woman in the world; abducted by Aphrodite and Paris, the act that started the Trojan War.

Homer (9th–8th? cent. B.C.E.) Greek epic poet and presumed author of the *Iliad* and the *Odyssey,* oral poems that were later written down and became the foundation of Greek literature and culture.

Horace Quintus Horatius Flaccus (65–8 B.C.E.); Roman poet.

Jove Chief ancient Roman god; analogous to the Greek Zeus; also called Jupiter.

Julia (39 B.C.E.–14 C.E.) daughter of Caesar Augustus; her adulterous behavior after an unwanted marriage eventually led to her exile.

Jupiter Chief ancient Roman god; comparable to the Greek Zeus; also called Jove.

Juvenal Decimus Junius Juvenalis (55 or 60–ca. 127 C.E.); Roman poet and satirist.

Lactantius Lucius Caecilius Firmianus Lactantius (ca. 240–320 C.E.); Latin church father and teacher of rhetoric.

Laura Real or imagined woman who inspired much of Petrarch's poetry; allegedly first seen by him in 1327 in the Church of Saint Clare in Avignon.

Leto Mythological Greek Titan; mother of Apollo and Artemis; also called Latona.

Livia Livia Drusilla (ca. 58 B.C.E.–29 C.E.); first Roman empress; married to and divorced from Nero, then married to Caesar Augustus.

Lucan Marcus Annaeus Lucanus (39–65 C.E.); Roman poet.

Muses Greek goddesses of music, the literary arts, and astronomy.

Narcissus In Greek mythology, a beautiful boy who spurned the love of the nymph Echo and whom the goddess Nemesis punished by causing him to fall in love with his own reflection.

Nemesis In Greek mythology, initially a goddess who allotted both happiness and misery, later the goddess who punished crimes.

Nero (37–68 C.E.) Roman emperor 54–68 C.E.

Numa Pompilius (8th–7th cent. B.C.E.) Second legendary king of early Rome; credited with founding nearly all of the earliest religious institutions of Rome.

Orcus Roman god of the underworld; equivalent to the Greek god Hades or Pluto; also called Dis.

Orpheus Mythological Greek poet married to Eurydice; when she died, he followed her to the underworld and won her back with his music, only to lose her again when he turned to look back at her against the gods' instructions.

Ovid   Pubilius Ovidius Naso (ca. 43 B.C.E.–17 C.E.) Roman poet; banished by Caesar Augustus and died in exile.

Palinurus   Pilot of Aeneas's ship in Virgil's *Aeneid.*

Paul, Saint   (ca. 10–67 C.E.) Christian apostle and author whose letters, canonized in the New Testament, are among the oldest extant Christian writings.

Peneus   In ancient mythology, a river god who was Daphne's father.

Peripatetics   Followers of Aristotle.

Philip   Philip II of Macedon (382–336 B.C.E.); ruled Macedon 359–336 B.C.E.; began the subjugation of Greece that was continued by his son, Alexander the Great.

Phoebe   Mythological Greek Titan; mother of Leto and grandmother of Apollo and Artemis.

Plato   (ca. 428–347 B.C.E.) Athenian philosopher, disciple of Socrates, and teacher of Aristotle; founder of the Academy, a school of philosophy near Athens that endured until the first century B.C.E..

Plutarch   (ca. 46–after 119 C.E.) Greek biographer and philosopher.

Publilius Syrus   (ca. 1st cent. B.C.E.) Roman author quoted by Aulus Gellius in *Attic Nights;* freed after arriving in Rome as a slave.

Pythagoreans   Followers of sixth-century B.C.E. Greek philosopher and mathematician Pythagoras who were prominent in southern Italy until the mid-fourth century B.C.E.; Pythagorean thought then diverged into a scientific branch and a religious branch.

Romulus   With his brother, Remus, legendary founder of Rome.

Sallust   Gaius Sallustius Crispus (ca. 86–34 B.C.E.); Roman historian and politician.

Scipio Africanus   Publius Cornelius Scipio Africanus (ca. 236–183 B.C.E.); Roman general and statesman who defeated Hannibal at Zama in 202 B.C.E.; the hero of Petrarch's *Africa*.

Seneca   Lucius Annaeus Seneca or Seneca the Elder (ca. 55 B.C.E.–39 C.E.); Roman rhetorician.

Seneca   Lucius Annaeus Seneca or Seneca the Younger (ca. 4 B.C.E.–65 C.E.); Roman Stoic philosopher and playwright.

Socrates   (ca. 469–399 B.C.E.) Athenian philosopher; developer of the Socratic method of inquiry and instruction, known through the writings of his disciple Plato.

Stoics   School of philosophy founded by Zeno of Citium ca. 300 B.C.E.

Suetonius   Gaius Suetonius Tranquillus (ca. 69–122 C.E.); Roman biographer and historian.

Terence   Publius Terentius (ca. 190–159 B.C.E.); Roman comic playwright.

Thais   (4th cent. B.C.E.) Athenian hetaera and mistress of Alexander the Great.

Tiberius   Tiberius Claudius Nero Caesar Augustus (42 B.C.E.–37 C.E.); second emperor of Rome (14–37 C.E.); son of Livia and Nero, adopted by Caesar Augustus.

Titus   Titus Flavius Vespasianus (39–81 C.E.); emperor of Rome 79–81; eldest son of Vespasian, brother of Domitian.

Venus   Roman goddess of love and mother of Aeneas.

Virgil   Publius Vergilius Maro (70–19 B.C.E.); Roman poet; author of the *Aeneid*.

Zeno of Citium   (ca. 335–263 B.C.E.) Greek philosopher; founder of Stoicism.

Zeus   Chief ancient Greek god; analogous to the Roman Jupiter or Jove.

A Petrarch Chronology
(1304–1374)

1304   Francesco Petrarca (in English, Petrarch) is born in Arezzo.

1312   Petrarch moves to Carpentras (just outside Avignon) and begins to study Latin with Convenevole da Prato.

1316   Petrarch begins to study law at the University of Montpellier.

1320   Petrarch continues to study law at the University of Bologna.

1325   Petrarch, in his earliest known book purchase, buys a copy of Augustine's *City of God*.

1326   Death of Ser Petracco, Petrarch's father; Petrarch returns to Avignon.

1327   Petrarch's alleged first encounter with Laura.

1330   Petrarch becomes a cleric; probably commits to celibacy.

1336   Petrarch's first trip to Rome.

1337   Petrarch begins his historical work *On Famous Men*.
Petrarch's son is born.

1338–
1339   Petrarch begins his epic poem *Africa*.

1341   Petrarch is crowned poet laureate in Rome. (April 8)

1342   Petrarch collects the first version of his *Rime sparse*.
Petrarch meets Cola di Rienzo in Avignon.

1343   Petrarch's daughter is born.
One proposed date for the first version of *The Secret*.

1345   Petrarch finds and reads some of Cicero's personal letters.

1347   First outbreak of the plague in Italy.
Cola di Rienzo comes to power in Rome; later abdicates.
One proposed date for the first version or revision of *The Secret*.

1348   Outbreak of the plague in Florence.

1353 Petrarch moves to Milan, with the ruling Visconti family as patrons.
One proposed date for revision of *The Secret*.

1354 Cola di Rienzo is killed in Rome.

1358 One proposed date for the final revision of *The Secret*.

1361 Petrarch moves to Padua with Francesco da Carrara as patron.
Petrarch moves to Venice as a guest of the city.
Petrarch's son dies from the plague.

1370 Petrarch moves to Arquà; continues to revise his writings.

1374 Petrarch dies in Arquà.

Questions for Consideration

1. The introduction to this volume argues that *The Secret* can be read as a humanist manifesto. What does this mean? Do you agree or disagree with this interpretation? Why?

2. After reading *The Secret* and studying later humanism, what do you think the relationship is between the humanist movement and the Renaissance?

3. Do you think that Petrarch deserves to be considered the first humanist? Why or why not? How does *The Secret* differ from later humanist writings?

4. What evidence do you see in *The Secret* of the new forms of political life that arose in Italy during the twelfth and thirteenth centuries?

5. Some scholars have argued that *The Secret* is a dialogue about reading and how to read. Others have argued that it is a dialogue about desire and its role in human life. Still others read it as a kind of autobiography. Find evidence in the text to support each of these views. What themes do you think are most central in *The Secret*?

6. *The Secret* was revised after the plague ("the black death") first swept through Italy. Do you see any evidence in *The Secret* of this devastating epidemic? Could you argue that *The Secret* is a response to the plague? Why or why not?

7. Historian Hanna H. Gray once characterized humanism as "the pursuit of eloquence." What do you think she meant by this? How is eloquence defined and discussed in *The Secret*? Do you think that the pursuit of eloquence was essential to Petrarch's humanism? Why or why not?

8. Why do you think Augustinus quotes so many pagan writers and comparatively few Christian writers in *The Secret*? Do Augustinus and Franciscus treat pagan and Christian writers differently? Does the dialogue take a position on the value of pagan literature to a Christian society?

9. Throughout the dialogue, Augustinus criticizes Franciscus both for his desire to please his friends and for his pursuit of fame. What connections do you see in the dialogue between friendship and fame?

10. In the first dialogue, when Augustinus is discussing desire, he insists on the difference between ability and volition: Whereas Franciscus says he *cannot* shed his unhappiness, Augustinus claims that he *will not* shed it. Why does Augustinus insist on this distinction? Why is he so attentive to the meanings and the differences in meaning of specific words when it comes to desire?

11. At one point in the second dialogue, Augustinus urges Franciscus to accept his fate as a human being. What is this fate? How does Augustinus define human nature? How does this definition of human nature fit in with your understanding of the aims of the humanist movement?

12. In the second dialogue, Augustinus uses a familiar list of seven deadly sins to evaluate Franciscus. In the third dialogue, Augustinus talks more specifically about Franciscus's peculiar failings—his love for Laura and his desire for worldly fame. How do these conversations differ? For example, do they differ in tone, in style of argument, or in their use of quotations?

13. Find the passages in *The Secret* where Franciscus interprets specific passages from Virgil's *Aeneid*. How would you characterize these interpretations? Does Franciscus seek to recover the meaning that Virgil intended to communicate, or does he use some other strategy? What function do these interpretations play in *The Secret*? What about the passages from Cicero's works? In general, what function do passages from other ancient authors play in *The Secret*?

14. What is Augustinus's view of Laura?

15. How does Augustinus define the relationship between the human body and the human soul? Why is this distinction important in the dialogue? How does the discussion of Laura relate to the distinction Augustinus has made between body and soul?

16. What do you think Franciscus means by the term *fortune*? How does his understanding of fortune relate to his quest for virtue and happiness? Does Augustinus share this understanding?

17. How do you interpret the end of *The Secret*?

Selected Bibliography

SELECTED TEXTS

Augustinus, Aurelius. *De civitate dei*. Edited by Dombart and Kalb. *Corpus Christianorum Series Latina* XLVII–XLVIII. Turnhout, 1955. Latin text of *The City of God*.

———. *The City of God against the Pagans*. Translated by David Wiesen. 7 vols. *Loeb Classical Library*. Cambridge, Mass., 1968. Latin text with English translation.

———. *Confessions*. Translated by William Watts. 2 vols. *Loeb Classical Library*. Cambridge, Mass., 1912. Latin text with English translation.

———. *Confessions*. Edited with commentary by James J. O'Donnell. 3 vols. Oxford, 1992 and 1997.

———. *Confessiones*. Edited by Verheijen. *Corpus Christianorum Series Latina* XXVII. Turnhout, 1981. Latin text of the *Confessions*.

Petrarca, Francesco. *Familiarium Rerum Libri*. Edited by V. Rossi and U. Bosco. Florence, 1933–42. Latin text of Petrarch's *Familiar Letters*.

———. "How a Ruler Ought to Govern His State." Translated by Benjamin Kohl. In *The Earthly Republic: Italian Humanists on Government and Society*. Edited by Benjamin Kohl and Ronald Witt with Elizabeth Wells. Philadelphia, 1978. English translation of letter to Francesco da Carrara.

———. *Letters on Familiar Matters*. Translated by Aldo S. Bernardo. Baltimore, 1985. English translation only.

———. *Letters of Old Age*. Translated by Aldo S. Bernardo, Saul Levin, and Reta A. Bernardo. Baltimore, 1992. English translation only.

———. *Opera*. 2 vols. Basel, 1554. Reprinted (facsimile) by Gregg Press, 1965.

———. *Opere latine di Francesco Petrarca*. Edited by A. Bufano. 3 vols. Turin, 1975. Latin text (with Italian translation) of *The Secret* and other works.

———. *Petrarch's Lyric Poems*. Edited and translated by R. Durling. Cambridge, 1976. Italian text of *Rime sparse* with English translation.

———. "The Ascent of Mont Ventoux" and "On His Own Ignorance and That of Many Others." Translated by Hans Nachod. In *The Renaissance*

Philosophy of Man. Edited by E. Cassirer, P. O. Kristeller, and J. H. Randall Jr. Chicago, 1948. English translation only.

SELECTED STUDIES IN ENGLISH

Baron, Hans. *Petrarch's Secretum: Its Making and Meaning.* Cambridge, Mass., 1985.

Brown, Peter R. L. *Augustine of Hippo.* Berkeley, 1969.

Brucker, Gene. *Renaissance Florence.* Berkeley, 1983 (reprint).

Burckhardt, Jacob. *The Civilization of the Renaissance in Italy.* Translated by S. G. C. Middlemore. New York, 1929.

Cosenza, Mario, ed. *The Revolution of Cola di Rienzo.* 2nd edition. New York, 1986. English translations of Petrarch's various writings about Cola di Rienzo.

Grafton, Anthony, and Lisa Jardine. *From Humanism to the Humanities: Education and the Liberal Arts in Fifteenth- and Sixteenth-Century Europe.* Cambridge, Mass., 1986.

Greene, Thomas. *The Light in Troy: Imitation and Discovery in Renaissance Poetry.* New Haven, 1982.

Hampton, Timothy. *Writing from History: The Rhetoric of Exemplarity in Renaissance Literature.* Ithaca, 1990.

Kahn, Victoria. "The Figure of the Reader in Petrarch's *Secretum.*" *Proceedings of the Modern Language Association,* 100 (1985): 154–66.

Kelley, Donald. *Renaissance Humanism.* Boston, 1991.

Kraye, Jill, ed. *The Cambridge Companion to Renaissance Humanism.* Cambridge, England, 1996.

Kristeller, Paul Oskar. *Renaissance Thought and Its Sources.* Edited by M. Mooney. New York, 1975.

Marsh, David. *The Quattrocento Dialogue: Classical Tradition and Humanist Innovation.* Cambridge, Mass., 1980.

Martines, Lauro. *Power and Imagination: City-States in Renaissance Italy.* New York, 1979.

Nauert, Charles. *Humanism and the Culture of Renaissance Europe.* Cambridge, England, 1995.

Quillen, Carol E. *Rereading the Renaissance: Petrarch, Augustine, and the Language of Humanism.* Ann Arbor, 1998.

Reynolds, L. D., and N. G. Wilson. *Scribes and Scholars: A Guide to the Transmission of Greek and Latin Literature.* Oxford, 1974.

Seigel, Jerrold. *Rhetoric and Philosophy in Renaissance Humanism: The Union of Eloquence and Wisdom, Petrarch to Valla.* Princeton, 1968.

Trinkaus, Charles. *The Poet as Philosopher: Petrarch and the Formation of Renaissance Consciousness.* New Haven, 1979.

Wilins, Ernest H. *Life of Petrarch.* Chicago, 1961.

Witt, Ronald. *In the Footsteps of the Ancients: The Origins of Humanism from Lovato to Bruni.* Leiden, 2000.

Index